;but God

# ;but God

*He is faithful in the midst of chaos.*

## Amanda Joy Harris

XULON ELITE

Xulon Press Elite
555 Winderley Pl, Suite 225
Maitland, FL 32751
407.339.4217
www.xulonpress.com

© 2024 by Amanda Joy Harris

All rights reserved solely by the author. The author guarantees all contents are original and do not infringe upon the legal rights of any other person or work. No part of this book may be reproduced in any form without the permission of the author.

Due to the changing nature of the Internet, if there are any web addresses, links, or URLs included in this manuscript, these may have been altered and may no longer be accessible. The views and opinions shared in this book belong solely to the author and do not necessarily reflect those of the publisher. The publisher therefore disclaims responsibility for the views or opinions expressed within the work.

Unless otherwise indicated,Scripture quotations taken from the Holy Bible, New Living Translation (NLT). Copyright ©1996, 2004, 2007 by Tyndale House Foundation. Used by permission of Tyndale House Publishers, Inc.

Scripture quotations taken from the New King James Version (NKJV). Copyright © 1982 by Thomas Nelson, Inc. Used by permission. All rights reserved.

Scripture quotations taken from The Message (MSG). Copyright © 1993, 1994, 1995, 1996, 2000, 2001, 2002. Used by permission of NavPress Publishing Group. Used by permission. All rights reserved.

Paperback ISBN-13: 978-1-66289-606-4
eBook ISBN-13: 978-1-66289-607-1

*To Jacob, Grace, Faith and Noah may you never have to experience the trials that made me who I am. May you always find value in yourself and your identity in Jesus.*

# Acknowledgements

**FIRST AND FOREMOST** I would like to thank God for gently urging me to write my story. I knew I had to get the events from my past out of my mind, but in all honesty once they came out, you could healed the space they occupied. Then you did something I never asked for, and made me the writer that I always dreamed about as a little girl.

Secondly to my best friend and husband Luke. You have always walked by my side and helped me through with your words of encouragement and wisdom. Thank you for praying over and protecting me while I had to break the chains of my past. I know that going through this was not easy, but it has been so worth it. Thank you for reminding me the purpose of what breaking free meant for our children.

Lastly thank you for my inner circle. Thank you for always being ready to pray and encourage when I doubted the worth of getting this book published. Thank you for painstakingly editing the copies I gave you and even questioning why I wrote what I wrote.

# Preface

**THIS BOOK IS** for all of those who suffered in silence and wanted to scream for help, only to learn that no one would listen. It is for those who longed for love only to be met with a leverage system of what will you give me if I love you. It is for those suffered at the hands of others who claimed to love you, and made you keep close mouthed to others at what was happening inside the interior of your home. It is for those who searched for someone who approved and accepted them, just to learn you would never measure up. It is for those who had to walk away, because you were at a hair's width away from losing sanity, only to be met with hate when you did. It is for those who carry the burden of trauma their entire life hoping to find someone to help you lay it down without judgement. Lastly it is for those who long for healing and don't think there is anyone who knows what you have been through, this book is for you.

# Table of Contents

Preface . . . . . . . . . . . . . . . . . . . . . . . . . . . . . . . . . . . . . . . . . . . . . . ix
Introduction . . . . . . . . . . . . . . . . . . . . . . . . . . . . . . . . . . . . . . . xiii
Chapter 1: **Childhood 0-2** . . . . . . . . . . . . . . . . . . . . . . . . . . . . 1
Chapter 2: **Childhood 3-6** . . . . . . . . . . . . . . . . . . . . . . . . . . . . 8
Chapter 3: **Childhood 6-10** . . . . . . . . . . . . . . . . . . . . . . . . . . 16
Chapter 4: **Childhood 11-14** . . . . . . . . . . . . . . . . . . . . . . . . . 33
Chapter 5: **Childhood 14-18** . . . . . . . . . . . . . . . . . . . . . . . . . 70
Chapter 6: **Adulthood - Overcoming My Childhood** . . . . . . . . 103
Chapter 7: **Restoration - My Testimony** . . . . . . . . . . . . . . . . 126

# Introduction:

**HEY, HOW ARE** you doing? That good huh? I know there must be a reason that you were drawn to this book. Could you be healing, and you are looking for similarities between your story and mine and what I did to heal? Or you saw this book, which reminded you about a dear friend who could benefit from reading it. Maybe, my dear, you are in your own personal hell and don't know how you will ever get past this. Whatever the case may be, please read this book. I understand that no two stories are the same, but they have similarities that connect us. I hope that by reading this book, you gain knowledge and insight into how trauma affects us in many ways. I know beyond a shadow of a doubt that there are ways that you have suffered that I never did. I hope we learn and lean into each other and, more importantly, on God. Part of my story is ugly, but it eventually became beautifully blessed. I know there were several times along the way that I was very tempted to give in and become just like them when the misery became too great to hold. I wanted to escape the pain of not being loved and cared for. But by the grace of God, I didn't give in. I moved towards God and am forever grateful for doing that. I look back now and see I was just one step, one decision away from a totally different life. Thank you, God, that I didn't take that step or make that decision.

;but God. In the English language, there are several different punctuations that I could begin that saying with. A comma was different from what I wanted because it breaks up sentences. A semicolon is a continuation of a sentence. Even though I know that is often associated with suicide, and while my story has that, I wanted it to become more. Each one of us has a sentence that sums up our lives. What if we decide to put ;but God at the end of it instead of a period? What if we allow God to make that continuation of our story?

**For instance:**

My story is one of horrible abuse and neglect, questioning love and losing trust in those around me; but God, through the chaos, walked with me every step of the way, ensuring I did not become crushed by my situation.

While that sentence doesn't entirely sum up my life, it brings me to this. What if we choose to let God finish each of our life stories and sentences? How would that change the outcome for each of us? It has taken me years to understand that God wanted me to share this story. I have fought against it because I didn't want to let the ugly out. I tried to hide it and the shame. I also didn't want to tell anyone what happened to me. The saying I always heard as a child was, "What happens in this house stays in this house." This was at the forefront of my mind. It was a battle to get past that. However, this book serves a dual purpose. With each word and chapter, I began to realize the healing that needed to happen. For example, when you cut your finger and become infected, you must clean the wound out and clear the infection before it can heal. God drew out the infection I had let fester with each written word over time. It was debilitating me and keeping me from living a full life. It was a pain that I continued to feel daily, and some days were horrible. I felt like I was being hit with waves of pain, moment after moment. It had to come out so I could view my life differently.

Please understand that this is my story of trauma; it is raw and unfiltered. This is the path I have walked to get through it. It is purely

*Introduction:*

to help others open their eyes to people around them and let them see one of two things. First, there are people in our lives who have suffered at the hands of others, or it could even be you. Secondly, how people react and see others might be a conditioned response that they have used to survive. Trauma, no matter how big or small, can manage our behavior. Often, it is beyond our control to stop what we are doing if we don't acknowledge or heal from it. As a trauma survivor myself, I have let my conditioned responses manage my behavior, and the outcome is not always good. As we can eventually leave those situations of trauma, there's this idea in our head that everything is fine. We fail to realize that this idea can ruin a relationship with loved ones. It can destroy our perspective on life and ruin our outlook because we are afraid to look past our past.

As trauma survivors, we have learned behaviors that become ingrained in us. Those behaviors are at the root of most of our problems and why we react the way we do. I expected my mother to be like my grandmother, who raised me for my first few years. Why did someone who fought to keep me react to me the way she did? The experiences and events that happened to me throughout my youth became ingrained in the person I became as an adult. Healing had to take place, and it would take a long time. If you are reading this book today, writing this book was a struggle to let my past out. I wanted to let people see what happened to me from childhood and part of my adulthood. So, I give this book to God. I will allow him to speak through me and reveal in you and in myself what I need to change and how growth is necessary. And yes, it can be painful, but there's good pain. We are evolving, cracking that hard outer shell, and growing.

**Disclaimer:** I am by no means a licensed professional. The experiences I write about are purely my own and can sometimes seem unimaginable. I have had enough life experience to warrant a PhD. I have instances burnt into my being that have tainted my outlook on how I see circumstances. I have had to unlearn these traits because they have made me miserable and have hurt the ones I love. At 42, I learned that I need to go backward to go forward. I want you to understand that I am a human being. I still deal with problems inside my mind, and I still do not have everything figured out. Mostly, it is safeguards that I have built to shield myself from those thoughts and feelings that produce memories. This book is to help you and me clean up our minds a bit so that we learn that we are no longer stuck in those situations and can take responsibility for our actions and move on to healing. We must look beyond what happened to us and try to remove that knee-jerk reaction to return there. Then, see what that reaction is doing to those around us. Yes, you read that right.

We can cause harm to others when we do not heal. I read a quote once that said if you do not heal from what hurt you, you will bleed on those who did not cut you. Our mind has neural pathways that will be forever part of our brain, and we cannot eliminate them. However, we can build new pathways and condition our minds to go around those things that will keep us stuck where we are in life. As ones who have dealt with trauma, we need to heal what hurt us. If we don't, we will always see others through the lens of our hurt. I also want you to know that this book deals not just with abuse. It also deals with traits we can develop that are not good either. Could these traits develop because of the trauma? It could be because we are human and want things the way we want them in every aspect of our lives. I am going to start from the beginning. It is not all roses; it is, in fact, quite the opposite, and it's heartbreaking and sometimes graphic. However, more than anything, I want you to see that you can heal with God leading the way. Our past has everything to do with our present expectations for our life. Whether you had trauma or a great childhood, both still shape you in ways that you do not truly realize or understand. In the

*Introduction:*

chapters of this book, I will go over the multiple phases of my life. I will add God's word to encourage you to always look to God and see how everything is orchestrated through Him.

# CHAPTER 1

# Childhood: 0-2 years.

**THIS IS NOT** the central part of our lives, but this is a vast area that we get shaped before we become adults. This is where we have the most influence placed on us. This is where we learn traits, characteristics, and personality that could be good or bad for us. This is where we pick up positive traits, such as learning to be optimistic. Or negative traits such as narcissism. I am unsure how I ended up as I am, but I am eternally optimistic. I want to see the good in everything. I want everything to turn out good. As I have learned from childhood, it does not always end up that way. I do not know much about my family history besides my bloodline and who we are. We have famous people as part of our bloodline, which is essential in my family, even more so than where we came from. I don't know if these characteristics I inherited are in my bloodline or if they are just something I have been blessed with. I was born in 1979. You would think I had a traditional family, mother, father, everything was good. Actually, it is quite the opposite. My mom grew up in a family of four siblings, two brothers, and two sisters. As far as I knew, she had a very stable upbringing. I am not sure what happened in her life to make her turn out the way she did. My family is closed-mouth about pretty much everything from the past. If she causes problems, then we are immediately to forgive her. Then we let her have her way to keep the peace. I know she was always at odds with one person or another in her family, much of her life, and mine. They do not talk about what happened in her youth. Everybody keeps emotions and past hurts held in.

To this day, I am not sure what happened in my mom's past or even my family's past. My mom had my brother and me five years apart. Due to uncertainty, she was involved with several men and could not share who our fathers were. I do not know the circumstances of my conception or birth because no one wants to talk about it. My mom has changed her story numerous times, so I do not know what to believe. I do know that my mom nearly died giving birth to me. I know my grandfather (Pap) told my mom she should give me up. It's heartbreaking to hear that coming from my mom; I often wondered if there was any truth to it because my Pap didn't act like he wanted to get rid of me when I was around him. I didn't get close to him, but he always went out of his way to take care of me. However, there were times that I wished she had given me to another family because of what I went through in my life. I wanted that fairy tale part of my life I always hoped for. But according to her, she fought my grandfather and insisted on keeping me.

My grandma instantly fell in love with me when I was brought home. She always reminded me of that when she told that story. I have a brother, Tim, and I didn't remember him much until I was 3 or 4. To this day, I don't have a close relationship with him, and I never really understood why. Having someone to lean on and talk to through these years would have been a great help. It could be that we are five years apart or did not mesh as people. It is hard for me to remember anyone other than my Grandma and Pap in the first two years of my life. We lived with my grandparents for a short time after I was born. But it seemed like my grandmother was the one who took care of us.

My mom always loved animals, and horses were always at the top of that list. That is where she poured out her affection. Years later,

*Childhood: 0-2 years.*

I learned that my mom did not have much to do with me and my brother when we were young. She worked at a racing barn, which bred Standardbred horses to cart race every week. She got to train the horses, meet famous people, and do what she loved. She worked very hard at that. I applaud that tenacity about her, but sometimes, I felt like we got the short end of her attention. The problem as I look back is that I should remember her taking care of me, and I don't. I can't remember her holding me or being in that part of my life. I remember my aunts, uncles, grandma, and grandpa, but not her. I am sure she was there, wasn't she? I would remember that, wouldn't I? I don't know if she was mentally or emotionally stable enough to have kids. Let alone try to raise us. Therefore, I never really had a relationship with her.

Growing up on a farm, you learn that the mother (speaking of the connection between animals) must imprint on the baby. This is so they can find each other should the mother and offspring separate. I hate to liken our relationship to that, but I did not have that with my mom during childhood or adulthood. I have always felt disjointed, like I was a part of her, but I did not belong to her. This led to other relationship issues as I grew up. The only thing we had in common was that we both loved animals, except the love she showed the animals created jealousy in me. She seemed never to be able to get enough either. I was always okay with one or two, but she always exceeded well past that. Eventually, this even caused relationship problems.

However, my grandmother was always there and ready to care for us during this stage. On my second birthday, I remember sitting at the head of the table in my little chair. I can vividly remember everyone around the table, my grandparents, aunts, and uncles, but I cannot remember my mom. She had to be there, should have been there. I cannot pull her out of that memory. Did she bake the cake? Or watching me from behind? I know that the mundane tasks in life fade into the background, so I hope she would have been there for something like a party. I want to put her in a good light but cannot remember her. Knowing what I know now, she was probably doing her own thing like always. I remember some gifts, like one my Aunt Deb made by crocheting. I appreciate that effort, but it was this bright red clown, and it was at least four feet tall. It scared the hell out of me at 2 years old. I remember jumping out of my chair and hiding under the table until Aunt Deb took it into another room. I know it was not her purpose to do that, but I still fear clowns to this day. Thanks, Aunt Deb!

Around this age, my mom met a man whom I called Dad, whose name was Tony. They married after two weeks, and we were whisked away from Grandma and her loving home. At this young age, you want things to be like they were with grandma because of how she cared for you, and your mind gets trained to know that. I remember crying a lot for Grandma during this time, but I would get smacked and told to shut up. Grandma was loving and made sure I had everything I needed. So that expectation and that schedule got moved to the side when my mom took us when she married Tony. Things just went downhill from there. My mom was severely abused. She was so scared and weak in her mind. Tony did everything short of killing her. I never saw what he did, but it could be heard as it echoed through the houses we lived in through the years.

I tried hiding under the bed in my room and covering my ears. The fighter in me wanted to help, but what could I do being so small? His abuse eventually passed over to me and my brother. My brother's abuse from Tony was both mentally and physically. I suffered several different types of abuse at the hands of this man. It was not fair. How could we go from the safe and loving environment at my grandmother's house to not knowing where our heads were going to lay at night or where food was going to come from. I remember that hollow hunger from that young age and how there never seemed to be enough when there used to be plenty. I often wonder how I turned out the way I am when my mom went in the other direction. I am not close to my brother, so I am unsure how he turned out; I know he is not like her. I have been around him enough as an adult to see that he chose a different path like me.

This all started at age two and went on to fourteen when my stepdad was part of the family dynamic. My mom eventually turned into an abuser as well. I loved them because I desperately hoped that emotion would get reciprocated. I expected my own mother to be just like my grandmother. Unfortunately, she was not. And yet again, I still questioned whether she was ready to commit to having a family and kids. I am unsure how my mom and stepdad got together or the story behind that. Again, nobody will share details with me. Some say they like met by an ad in the newspaper, I am not sure. Then, two short weeks later, they were married. There is insufficient time to figure out this man's character or tendencies.

## Pivot Point

No matter how hard we try, we cannot look at someone else and think they will be like what we are used to or know. We must take them at face value. We cannot expect that person to treat us with the best intentions, even if it is a family member. Nor can we look at them and think they are just like the last one. In this instance, I had no choice but to go with my mom because I was her child, I did not know her, and I did not know what my life would bring. We need to be careful not to view others through the lens of previous people and what they did for us or to us. Not one person is the same. God did not intend for my life to be lived this way. He does not want any of his children to suffer at the hands of another. If you truly love someone, you will care for them and hold their best interests at heart. That is the way that we are programmed by God. As a young child, I had a right to a loving childhood. That is our alienable right when we are born. There is nothing wrong with expecting that type of love in every relationship, especially with God. There is nothing wrong with knowing your worth. Where the fault lies is in the choices that are made and the aftermath of those choices. I was helpless in the situation my mom had chosen for herself. That choice would affect me for the rest of my life.

> **Jeremiah 1:5**: *"Before I formed you in your mother's womb, I chose you. Before you were born, I set you apart. I appointed you to be a prophet to the nations."*

God knew me and chose me before I was born. As hard as it is to think about, He knew I would go through these things in my life. I know it is sad and heartbreaking. Could he have stopped all of this? Yes, He is that powerful, but that also takes away our free will. Everything we go through is at his command. Still, we choose to disobey His commands freely. In any case, we also must deal with the aftermath and blast radius of our choices and decisions. Our decisions affect everyone and everything around us, no matter how innocent we are.

Just like I cannot remember my mom early on in my life. No matter how hard I try, I cannot see her face caring for me. It is my grandma, aunts, uncles, and even my Pap. So, in my mind, I asked, was she even there for me? I know that my grandma took the most care of me in those first 2 years, but did my mom take advantage of my grandparents and leave me with them? Oh, God, there are so many questions that I want answers to. Every child should have the right to expect a good childhood. Unfortunately, it does not always happen that way. Should my mom have listened to my grandfather and given me up? There are days I wish she had, especially with what happened in my life. I must cling to the fact that my life, no matter the trauma I went through, has a purpose. I would not have the life I have now if she had given me up; however, those are things I do not know, and I must sit with that. There is one thing I know the answer to: even though God allowed my mother to make those choices, He still walked me. Every day, he walked with me, and even though He allowed the choices that my mom and stepdad made, He protected my heart and mind and shielded them from the abuse.

## CHAPTER 2

# Childhood 3-6

**TONY DID NOT** let us stay in Pennsylvania for long before he moved us to Missouri. I am sure I had turned 3 by this time. I did not know what was happening to my mom. The abuse that she endured was done to her behind closed doors and at night while we were sleeping. Tony was not a good man at his core. I fully believed that he suffered PTSD from Vietnam, and that heightened his abuse of all of us. Tony had good qualities like providing for the family and making sure we had a roof over our heads and money for food, most of the time. Past that, he expected us to wait on him hand and foot and to be slaves in our own household. I did not have to do much at this age except look cute, smile when Tony asked, and sit on his lap whenever he wanted. He always wanted to see me smile. Even when I couldn't, he would force me. As a child, I was known as pretty and was told that every time we were out in public. My grandmother said I needed to be a model or put in acting. None of that ever happened, though. To Tony, I was his princess, and he often demanded that I be dressed like one. When Tony wasn't around, I was dressed in clothes I could get dirty, and I was delighted. I realize now that he was grooming me for things that would come later when I was older.

Tony created an ever-growing rift between my mom and me. I received a lot of attention from him in those early days and on. I was looking for someone to fill the void left by my grandparents, and he did that for a time. There is an ache in my heart now as I see the resentment my mom must have felt towards me. I received royal treatment while she and my brother had to jump at every command from him. What they did not understand was that I was a prisoner just like them. I was not allowed to be a normal kid and play when he was home. Sitting on his lap was sometimes all I was allowed to do. I would often have to sit there as he got served beer and alcohol and smell him as he got drunk. I desperately sought love and affection, and he filled that void, even though the love I thought I was getting would eventually become tainted.

We had moved to a small farm in rural Missouri, so keeping clean was not an option, but I did try. I remember we had a brick house and a farm with suitable acreage and peach trees. Eventually, I got good at not getting hurt or getting too dirty. I learned how to saddle and ride the horses and ponies by myself. I remember that there was a donkey in the field next door to us that I became good friends with. He would "heehaw" at me whenever I came out of the house. Animals became my most cherished friend because mom did not take me to many places away from home. I did not have many toys; I remember this grungy stuffed bear I talked to, my favorite Velveteen Rabbit book, and my little ponies.

I had many books and would line them up for roads that the ponies could run down or read when they weren't used for roads. I could read by the age of 3, having been taught by Tony while sitting on his lap. I had books on tape and learned to read from those as well. My brother had a lot of toys and seemed to have more than me. I would often sneak into his room and play with them when he was at school, but he always knew and would get mad at me. He would always tattle on me, and I would get swats from my mom when Tony wasn't around. I was not allowed to ride or play outside when Tony was home. So, I was a tomboy part of the time, climbing trees, jumping hay bales, and making a good mess of myself. The other, I was a perfect princess, not allowed to get dirty or hurt myself. I know that there were times during these young years that I had skinned knees. I faintly remember my mom suffering at the hands of this man because his perfect angel got hurt. Lord, I know she must have tried because I eventually started to feel the end of a peach limb or Tony's extra belt. Could they not understand that I wanted to play and have fun getting dirty?

I learned during this time of life, I loved to ride horses. I had so much freedom while in the saddle. I could go and do what I wanted while on horseback. This was one of the things that my mom and I had in common. She put me on a horse when I was 18 months old, and I was a natural at it. She proudly shared that with everyone she met. At this age, I could not do much with a horse other than be placed in the saddle and told to hang on. It was the one thing my mom and I enjoyed and shared early on in my life. Later in life, however, horses became a way for me to escape the pain. During our rides, she seemed to like me, even possibly love me. She would smile and challenge me to races, and we would ride all over the countryside. We would race each other, giggle, and laugh all the way to the barn. I often wished that those times wouldn't end. I knew that we both needed that, and I desperately clung to the mom she was when we rode horses, wishing above all else that she would stay that way. Eventually, the ride would end, and the carefree mom with it. There was always a noticeable change when her feet hit the ground from the stirrups. Why did it have to be this way? Why couldn't she love me when we were all prisoners here?

At the age of 4, I was taken to kindergarten, but I did not know what that was. My mom really did not speak of it, so I was not familiar with what it was. Thanks to the time I spent sitting on Tony's lap, I had been taught to read and write. I did not interact well with other children or adults, so this was foreign. Imagine my fear when she introduced me to my teacher and then left. I was horrified and cried and sat in the corner. I did not know how to interact with children my age. Everything about this place scared me. I understand the teacher was great, but I needed to gain social skills and learn how to communicate with people and animals outside my family.

I was not a bad kid in school; I just kept to myself. I often told my mom that I feared school and wanted to stay home, and I could learn everything there. I could read and write better than the kids in the classroom, and I was bored. I got in trouble because I would finish my work and then start fiddling with the stuff on my desk. I loved to draw, and that is what I would do, and I was quiet. However, that distracted the other kids, and they started asking questions about what I was doing. So, I got tattled on a lot that year and the consecutive years after because I would finish everything quickly. Recess was not a great time for me either. I did not get along with the girls well and was not allowed to play with the boys. I would often sit and play on the grass or build mini villages with sticks that held my imaginary friends. In the afternoons, I would sometimes ride the bus home alone; more times than I could count, the bus driver did not know where I lived. So that was added to my fear of being at school that I would never get back home.

My favorite part of the day was when I went to my after-school program and got to stay with the daycare worker. I cannot remember her name, but she left a significant imprint on me. As soon as I got off the bus there, she would come up and hug all of us, and I felt like she held on to me just a little longer than anyone else. She was such a light in the darkness for me. She made sure we had our snacks and would listen to how our day went and then invited all of us to play with her. I wouldn't speak much to her, and I cried a lot about not wanting to return to school. If it was my choice, I would always stay there with her. She was so much fun. Part of the time, we stayed indoors and played board games, read books, or drew pictures. While I liked those times, I loved when she would go outside with us, too. One of my favorite things with her was going on an "imagination" walk. She would take us in small groups through the neighborhood, and the path was always the same. It would go through places with houses, and then we would end up at this huge church.

One day, I remember we were knights and making our way back to the castle to protect the land of evildoers. The housing was the villages under our protection, and we would ask everyone if they needed help. That huge church was our castle, but before we got to it that day, we had to fight the dragon invading it. She removed sticks from the nearest tree and handed us our swords. We fought a courageous battle with her leading the charge. When the battle was finished, the king of the castle gave us commanding positions in his army the highest honor he could bestow. I would look at her with awe and wonder, willing myself to be like her when I was older. Everyone needs someone like her in their lives because she made my days so much brighter.

Shortly after that time, we moved to Georgia. My brother and I had the opportunity to go to my Grandma and Pap's before that for the summer. I remember she had such a massive house with a well-manicured lawn, which seemed like a mansion. There were fruit trees and flowers everywhere, and Grandma always had a vegetable garden. I was treated like a normal kid and felt so loved here. I was allowed to be a kid and get as dirty as I wanted, even though I would always have to take a shower or bath afterward. It was a treasured time for me because I got one-on-one attention from Grandma, who became my best friend. She would take me shopping, to the library, and to the swimming pool a time or two. The library was always a hit for me because it was huge and had all the kids' books I could ever want. However, my favorite was when she would take me to the ice cream stand.

I would get a vanilla and chocolate swirl dipped in sprinkles. To this day, I still eat sprinkles on my ice cream, which always has a hint of nostalgia. We would sneak into the kitchen at night to get butter pecan ice cream and add a dollop of peanut butter to the top. One of her favorite things was to have Pap take us out to eat. Bob Evan's and Denny's were her favorites. At one time, they had delicious food. She would also take us to the dollar store. Back then, it was a great store; she would give each of us five dollars, and we would find incredible treasures. We would often get kites, huge styrofoam planes, and those bouncy balls that you would bounce off the floor as hard as possible to see how high they would go. Those were such good times.

It was a wonderful reprieve for us despite the shortness of it. Sadly, it would always come to an end each summer, and we had to go back home. Except home was never where we had left it. My home was moved every summer starting at this point, and it became hard to feel I belonged anywhere. It was always hard to leave Grandma, and it got more challenging each time. She and Pap made me feel so loved and cherished. I was well-fed and allowed to be a kid with them. When I went back home, none of this would happen. I would get such a pit in my stomach on the road home. When we arrived in Georgia, I realized I would never see that lovely woman at the after-school program. She gave me such hope and inspiration. I was so heartbroken that I could never say goodbye to her. This would become the norm in my life until I was 12. My life was constantly uprooted over and over again. Friends and routines were made and lost within a year. Every year, I would have a break during the summer, and then I would have to face all new faces and places when I returned to wherever home would be for the next year.

## **Pivot Point:**

An unrealistic mantle was placed on me as a child. To always wear dresses and look like a little princess. To stay clean when we lived on a farm. To always be at Tony's beck and call. I was so young, and so many restrictions were placed on me. It was unfair for my mom to swat my bottom because I wanted to play outside and get dirty, just wanting to be a kid. Tony would not allow me or my mom to be social, and I would only really learn how to be friends with people once I was older, and even now, it is still tricky. These unfair expectations of me would be something that I would have to break in my mind when I was older. Kids will be kids, and putting them on a pedestal not made for them will always cause conflict. Not to mention that they will struggle with burdens that were not theirs to carry. Tony placed me on a pedestal of being a princess, and I did not want to be there. I wanted to play outside in the muck and mud of the farm freely without second-guessing my every move and what wrath I would face should I choose to do what I wanted. I wanted Tony to place Mom on that pedestal because she needed to be there, not me. I also wanted to be loved by my mom all the time and not just when we were riding horses. God made me for a purpose, and this was not it.

> *Do not withhold good from those to whom it is due when it is in your power to act.* **Proverbs 3:27**

This verse entirely sums up the light the after-school program lady and my grandmother shared with me. They were my oasis in the desert. It was so good during this period that I had someone who would allow me to be a kid. Through this time, I would struggle to learn who I was. I am so thankful for that sweet lady at the after-school program that would hold me extra tight on my hard days.

Being in her presence was the one part of the day that I would look forward to. In her presence, I found rest and reassurance. God knew I needed that sweet lady during those short years. The simple act of her allowing me to stretch my character and imagination in that time would be things I would cling to later. I learned that I could have individuality even when pigeonholed into something I did not want to be. Spending the summers with my grandma was also good because she let me talk and have conversations with her in ways my mom should have. Even in all this, God placed people where I needed them, even when life wasn't fair and I sought rescue.

# CHAPTER 3

# Childhood 6-10

**WE MOVED AWAY** from everything I knew repeatedly and would continue until I was 11 to 12 years old. I was not told why we always had to move, but it happened year after year. Everything would constantly be rearranged and uprooted when I got home from Grandma's after summer. I never knew what to expect when I returned. It was during this time that I got my faithful companion, Smokie. I loved that German shepherd mix so much. He went everywhere with me and kept me safe as much as possible. He was the one I could tell my problems to, and I often cried into his fur when days were terrible.

To this day, I still remember Smokie's smell of dog and pine trees. He would always greet me with such jubilance, and it did not matter if I was gone five minutes or all summer; he would run to me. I wish that my parents would have shown even a quarter of that love to me growing up and to make me feel wanted. I loved him more than anything in my world then because he loved me just as much. At this point, Mom was becoming more open about what she thought of me, especially since Tony spent a lot of money on me and got me a princess bedroom suite with a four-poster bed with a canopy and everything pink. The problem was that I never asked for or even wanted those things. I was told I would get them from Tony, so I did. I hate to admit it, but I started using my ability to bend Tony's will to get what I wanted. I wasn't a selfish child, but if I wanted something like a toy or to leave a place I didn't like, I would play with Tony's nature and how he treated me to get what I wanted. I knew in the back of my mind that it was a mistake to do that, but I did play that card against my Mom because of how she treated me. I knew it was a mistake because Tony started to use it to bargain with me.

I would have to smile, sit on his lap, be a good little girl, and not get in trouble. That meant that I would not be able to do anything because Mom was always looking for ways to tattle on me, so mostly, I had to sit at Tony's feet and play quietly, using my imagination of how a loving father would treat me. I was a prisoner in the household just my cage was pretty and glistened with forced goodness. Because I was treated this way, I did not have a good relationship with anyone in the household. This was also the time that she would openly display affection to Tim in front of me and would look right at me and say how much she loved him. I would feel great pain when she did that, and tears would burn in my eyes, but I couldn't let them fall. It would have been easier to have been stabbed by her than it was to watch her show love to Tim. I had to choke back the tears sitting at Tony's feet because I wasn't allowed to be anything other than happy while there. Once released from my spot, I often went to my room and cried until I had nothing left.

Tony started truck driving during this time and was gone a lot. Which was a great relief for all of us. My Mom would let me make a mess of myself, and if I got hurt, she would remind me that Tony would hear about it when he got home. It was also during this time that I began to be physically and sexually abused by Tony. The physical started pretty much after my Mom began to tattle on me. Tony would get tired of hearing it and start smacking me across the face or hitting other parts of my body. I was not a terrible or badly behaved kid. I was like every other kid in my era who wanted to play outside, ride my bike, climb a tree, and so on. I was quiet and kept to myself, and I wasn't disrespectful. I was generally a good kid. However, if I did something the slightest bit wrong, I was tattled on and then beaten by the person who treated me like a princess. My Mom would purposefully put me on horses that were not broken for a kid to ride to see if I would get hurt. I was between 6 and 10, not something I would have done with my children. If I got hurt, I would have to cover it up and not cry because I was going to get beat by Tony for getting hurt. Do you know how hard it was for me to cover that up? When a part of your body is throbbing and hurting so bad that all you want to do is cry? But you can't because your Mom was watching for tears to say something that would cause even more pain. I can't tell you how many times I got smacked across the face for getting myself hurt at her hands. I got on those horses because I desperately wanted her approval. I desperately wanted her to love me like she loved Tim. But if I got hurt, she would act like nothing happened, and then I would get double for my trouble when Tony got back home. This is also where I would learn that my Mom loved getting attention. Tattling on me was a way for her to get attention from Tony. If I could stay on the green broke horses, she would get attention from the men around the sale barn she worked at. This part was income for me because I would ride the horses being sold. After all, they were "kid broke," and the people selling would spot me a 5 or 10-dollar bill. Little did the buyers know that I was a seasoned rider. Looking back now, I cringe because of the lie and how many people may have been hurt because the horse was not as broken as it was said.

My Mom loved the attention of others and their praises of me. At my core, I was a good and intelligent kid. When I got into the gifted program in 3rd grade because I had an 8th-grade reading level, she would get attention from the teachers on how good of a parent she was and how bright I was. Another time, when I cut the skin open

## Childhood 6-10

above my eyebrow from a rabbit cage while I was trying to catch a loose rabbit for her, she took me to the emergency room. When we got back to one of the rooms, and the doctor was sewing me up, she passed out. Now, I have seen my Mom touch some gross and disgusting stuff, and she never passed out before. The doctor literally had to stop what he was doing and help the nurse get her off the floor. She had a way of getting attention when she wanted to. She did this time and time again. Every time I needed medical attention, she would get hurt somehow. She would "accidentally" hurt her wrist and her back or have an anxiety attack.

This seemed to be her habit when I got hurt, except for a time when she put me on a neighbor's horse that wasn't broken to ride. Everything started out like a typical ride. The horse was a little skittish and jumped at everything. I was scared because the horse was green, broke, and had only been ridden twice. I knew this was going to be an explosive combination. The horse seemed to sense that I was uncertain of her, but I always had a calming nature with horses, and soon I soothed her. We were having a good time with everyone until the horse I was riding got near another horse that didn't like her, and she got kicked. The young horse reared up so violently that it fell over backward on top of me, knocking me unconscious and dislocating both my shoulders. At that moment, I cannot begin to explain to you the fear that entered my body when I realized what was going to happen. To this day, I can vividly remember the horse's head hitting mine and then the both of us falling backward, and then sheer blackness. In normal circumstances, it would be expected that I would have been rushed to the hospital or an ambulance called, except nothing happened that way. I don't remember much about how everything happened, but I didn't wake up with medical personnel all over me.

I was just left on the floor of the neighbor's living room until I came to, in horrendous pain, and couldn't use my arms to sit up. I cried out in panic and pain, and no one came. I could hear my Mom outside talking to the neighbor about what she should do. Thinking back now, it should have been simple, take me to the hospital, but she didn't. She made me sleep on the floor in her bedroom where she could watch over me. I could not do anything on my own, had no use of my arms, and my head throbbed horribly. I threw up so many times that night and into the next day that I just ended up sleeping next to the toilet. I could not use my arms, and doing simple things like going to the bathroom was painful, and my Mom didn't help me with that. I felt like I was dying, and no one would help me. The next-door neighbor visited a few times to check on me, asking Mom if I had been taken to the doctor. I don't know what was said, but eventually, she quit coming by. I was eight years old when this happened to me. To this day, I still have a rotated collarbone on one of my shoulders, and they always ache. It took me weeks to gain use of my arms again. It was like trying to move your arm when it is asleep. They were heavy, and it was tiring. I was sent to school while one was still healing, and I had to hold that arm one up with the other. Mom didn't get me a sling to hold it in place. Teachers would ask how I was doing, and that is as far as it went. I wanted to scream at them and ask if they cared. I was not okay! Could they not see that? It took a lot of healing to get over the concussion, as well. My head always felt like it was swimming. I could not concentrate in school because my head hurt most of the time, and my grades suffered. I got removed from the gifted reading program because I fell behind in school. That program meant a lot to me, so this was like a final blow to an already broken body.

It took me years to recover from that accident. Mom never told Tony what happened. Thankfully, he was not home much during this time. My room became the only place I felt safe within the walls of that home, and even then, it wasn't very safe. I kept to myself mainly after this. I only came out of my room when I had to sit with Tony.

## Childhood 6-10

I lost interest in reading because it was too hard to concentrate anymore, and my head throbbed when I tried to read.

After this event in my life, Tony started to sexually abuse me. I hurt all the time and couldn't move quickly, and he would catch me as I was going out of the door trying to get away from him. Tony would grab me by my arms, sling me back toward the living room, and make me wait on him hand and foot as I winced in pain. I couldn't cry out because then he would hit or smack me, making the pain worse in my already battered body. He liked to wait until Mom went to work or town and leave me alone with him. He would fondle me and tell me not to tell anyone, or he would beat me. I soon learned the pattern of what he was doing, and I would try to stay around my brother or play outside, away from the house. If it was raining, I would go to my room and lock the door, trying to put a barrier between him and me and protect myself in any way I could. I even took Smokie in there, hoping he would protect me. However, Tony took advantage of the fact that no one in the house would help me and did what he wanted. When I finally mustered up the courage to tell Mom the way I was being abused. She looked directly at me and told me I was lying. I begged for her to help me, but she would shake off my pleas and cries for help and turn her back on me. Even though I was heartbroken at her saying I lied, I clung to her, crying desperately, trying to get through to her. I even tried to write a letter to my grandma for help, but my Mom tore it up right in front of me and said I was not allowed to say anything to Grandma. I had absolutely no one to reach out to. I felt so helpless and abandoned that I couldn't even make friends because I didn't want them to learn of the shame I carried. People that should have cared for me were doing everything in their power to destroy me.

What was a saving grace during this time, and I'm not sure why it happened, was that I got to spend one whole year with my grandparents. We had moved to a new place again and were waiting for a house to be built. We moved specifically to this land so that Mom would have a place to keep horses, even though it did not have a proper place to live. The four of us lived in a 10ft travel trailer with no bathroom or way to meet basic needs. I would go days without being able to bathe. I hated using the makeshift outhouse, so I would hold it until I got to school and not drink much in the evening when I got home. Weekends were hard, but I did my best to get through. If it was warm, we could bathe in the wash tub outside.

Looking back at this, it seemed like we were so poor. However, Tony worked, so we had money and horses, and they had a place to live. I had nowhere inside to protect myself from Tony anymore. Fortunately, there were a lot of places to hide outside on that property. While the house was being built, it came about that we were going to stay at our grandparents' house for the school year. I often wondered if the school got word of our living conditions or Grandma did. Either way, it was a godsend because it had been a couple of years since I could see Grandma since the horse accident. I remember packing what little clothing I had in a small bag. Gone were the nice things that I once had. During this time, I wore dirty, ill-fitting clothing that was too small. If I said anything about needing new clothes, I would get yelled at and smacked across the face. We had luxuries like brand-new saddles and expensive horses, even though we couldn't dress nicely to ride them.

When our grandparents picked us up, I remember Pap looking at me and asking if that was all I had to bring. I remember in times past that I would have 1 or 2 bags just stuffed full, but not this time. All I had were dirty, dingy clothes stuffed into a threadbare bag. I felt so ashamed and couldn't explain what had happened. I could only nod and not look at Pap so he wouldn't see the tears. We both must have looked awful standing next to them when we checked into the hotel later that evening. I remember Grandma asking about a washer, dryer, and a place to buy clothes. She took all our clothes and washed them and then gave a list to Pap to go and buy. When he returned, he handed Tim and me a large bag. When I opened mine, tears came to my eyes. New jeans, shirts, sweaters, underwear, socks, and shoes were in that bag. I wanted to thank them but could only look at them in amazement. Grandma said to go and take a shower and put on the new clothes so we could go to dinner. That shower was the best feeling that I had felt in a long time. I imagined that I must have washed off several months of dirt. Then, that feeling was surpassed by wearing clothes that fit. I felt normal if that's the word for it. I was so grateful for what they did for me.

I did not talk much the whole trip to their house, which was a two-day trip, and then it took me a little bit after we arrived. I had so much I wanted to tell them, but I couldn't get it to come out of my mouth. I remember them commenting when they thought I was asleep that first night and wondered what had happened and how they missed us talking. I wanted desperately to tell them, but I was so scared that Tony would find out and beat me. All I could do was let the tears silently fall as I fell asleep. They did not know how relieved I was to be away from Mom and Tony for a while. To know that I would be loved and taken care of. To take a bath or go to the bathroom freely. I could act like I was normal and do what I wanted. To not get tattled on and then beat when I got hurt. I wanted to scream and let them know how much I had gone through, how broken I was at the age of ten, if I could have just told them. That year, it was such a wonderful time to spend with them after what I had been through. Grandma enrolled me and Tim in school, but I didn't start immediately. It seemed that Grandma sensed that I had something wrong.

At this time, I was still getting headaches and still had a hard time concentrating, and I wasn't talking much, either. Like all the other new schools I started at, I was scared and shy, even standoffish. The people at that new school were amazing and treated me like one of their own. I felt like I had an identity in that school. Everyone knew me and called me by name. I learned many things and participated in gymnastics, track, and softball. This was the first time I got to participate in anything like that. I was forced to always come home when I was with my parents. It was also the first time I got to have Christmas with my grandparents and see snow during the holidays. Grandma also started taking me to church, and I got saved that summer while watching Billy Graham on TV. I didn't know what it all meant exactly, but I felt better than I had in a long time.

However, as the year went on, the closer it got for us to return home. It often felt like I was in a ticking time bomb that would explode at any minute. I felt so much anxiety over going back home. I begged Grandma to keep us, leveraging that I would be a good girl if only she would keep me as her daughter. She asked me why I was so scared to return home, but I still couldn't bring myself to tell her. I didn't want to leave people who had become my friends because I had some for once. It was heart-wrenching to think about leaving. I was growing and thriving there. I was so scared to go back to Mom and Tony. Scared that everything would be just like it was. Grandma just kept reassuring me that maybe things had changed and I needed to give it a chance. At this time in my life, I had given Mom and Tony so many chances, and I got abused because of it. I would have to stay on guard and erect a wall to protect myself again. Not that being a child could I protect myself from them. I felt like the days were counting down to my doom.

With all the begging and pleading, we were sent home anyway. To be honest, it wasn't horrible when we went back. Things were good for a while; we had a new house built and room to spread apart and isolate ourselves. I found an unfinished area in my room with a hole in the wall, opening to a storage area in the attic. It was small, and only I could get to it. I'm not sure my parents knew about it, but I pushed my dresser in front of the hole so it stayed covered. Gone were the days when I felt safe inside our house. That place became where I would go when I was alone with Tony. I had blankets, pillows, stuffed animals, clothes, drinks, snacks, and anything I thought would prove helpful if I had to hide for an extended period.

Going to the bathroom was an issue, but I learned how to silently push the dresser aside and sneak quickly to the bathroom. Little did I know how useful those skills would become in the coming days. Thoughts kept coming to me that I needed to prepare for something, and I couldn't grasp it. I started sneaking food and drinks to that secluded area like a squirrel preparing for winter. I had a backpack full of clothes, shoes, toilet paper, bandages, and anything I thought I could use. It would be my end if Mom or Tony ever found that spot.

Most of the year, things went well until spring break. I remember we were left home with Tony because he wouldn't return to work until the following week. I went into that secret place every day Mom went to work or left for town. I stayed in my safe place where I did not have to be near the people who hurt me. I'm unsure how anything started, but I could hear Tony roaring downstairs. After so many months of holding it in, his voice shook the entire house to the rafters. The next thing I knew, I could hear my brother getting the brunt of Tony's blows, and I felt each one and jumped as if it were happening to me. I heard Tim screaming, knocking over chairs in the kitchen, and trying to get away from Tony in any way possible. I heard the back door open, and Tim had made it outside, still screaming and running away from the house. It was one thing for me to be beaten, but to hear my brother getting it done to him made me want to throw up. I cried quietly into the bear I was clutching for dear life, praying that Tony would not find me. I heard him stomping up the stairs, yelling as he came.

I prayed against the acid rising in the back of my mouth that I could become invisible and disappear. He came towards my room, and I could hear his footsteps as he neared. He was screaming my name and roaring in anger. I held my breath so that my whimpers would not be heard. When he realized that I wasn't going to come out, he then took it upon himself to utterly destroy my room, throwing profanities and my things everywhere. I could hear toys breaking and books ripping as everything was thrown around my room. When that ended, he moved on to my brother's room, also causing destruction in there.

The chaos continued throughout the house until I heard him exit the front door and speed away in his truck, throwing gravel as he went. I really hoped that Tim found a place to hide quickly. It took hours for me to grow the courage enough to peek out of the hiding place, but the urge to use the bathroom was overpowering. I was barely able to push the dresser out of the way because there was carnage everywhere, and my desk and mattress were pinned up against it. As soon as I was out of safety, every sense became heightened, and every creak of the house was heard. I made it to the bathroom and back as quickly as possible, hoping against everything that Tony would not return to find me outside that place. This was the reason that I did not want to leave the safety of my grandma's house. This is why I begged her to keep me. The only safety I had now was that hole in the wall the builders left behind. I stayed in my secret place for hours, wishing everything would return to how it was yesterday. I sat there rocking back and forth, waiting for it all to end.

It seemed like a bad dream, but I could not wake up. I fell asleep eventually because I wore myself out with the crying. I was awakened by an engine pulling up to the house. My body instantly tensed in fear, and I curled into a ball to protect myself. I held my breath and strained to hear who it might be. Desperately hoping it wasn't

Tony and desperately hoping it was someone to help remove me from this hell. I heard someone downstairs trying to open the front door, pushing through the destruction everywhere, and cursing. It was Mom. Any hope I had fell with her coming through the front door. I soon heard her crying and later found out that Tony had killed one of the cats and one of the dogs. How could one person cause all this?

Not a second later, I heard her yelling for Tim, screaming at the top of her lungs, inside and out. I waited for her to call my name, but she never did. I wanted so badly to come out of my hiding place and say here I am and scream at her for how horrible everything was, but I just couldn't. I couldn't reveal myself; I didn't feel safe with her either. So, I stayed where I was. Mom spent most of the night cleaning up and crying, but she never left to look for Tim or come upstairs. She never called the police to report him missing or tell them what Tony had done. I slept intermittently through the night, never restful because I kept listening for Tony to return. He didn't return that night. I woke up well before dawn, mostly because I felt an urging to find Tim. He could be really hurt or at least hungry and cold. I had no idea where he went and hoped God would help me find him. We weren't the best siblings, but he was still my brother; someone needed to find and help him.

I pulled out unnecessary items and rearranged what I had in my backpack so I had room to get him some clothes and shoes if I could make it to his room undetected. I silently rushed to his room listening, the whole time for movement downstairs. The only one that noticed me was the other cat that ran and hid during the chaos. The cat rubbed against me, and I almost lost the last shred of courage as tears rushed to my burning eyes. She understood the horror I had witnessed and how scary it was to be in that house then. I wanted so badly at that moment to give in and sob on the floor of the mass destruction that was his room. One driving thought broke through,

Tim needed someone, even if it would only be me. I grabbed some clothes and shoes, shoving them into my full bag. The biggest challenge was to get downstairs and out one of the doors.

On the landing of the stairs, I sat and waited in the shadow. I strained to hear if Mom was awake. The cat had followed me and sat staring at me, almost as if wondering what the plan was. A loose board on one of the steps would squeak if I stepped on it; I needed to be careful. That cat must have known what I was thinking, so she darted ahead and went down the steps. She hit the step with the loose board, and I heard my Mom in her room. That's when I listened to the cat start meowing, running to Mom's room. While the cat distracted Mom, I took my chance to get to the back door because it was the closest. Once outside with the door firmly closed, it occurred to me that I didn't have a plan past to get out of the house. Now what? I kept thinking that I needed to go where we rode our bikes. There was a place on the land with short hills and valleys that we would spend hours riding up and down. That was my direction, except I went through the woods, which was slower than the road because I wanted to avoid being seen.

I went slowly, still not wanting to be heard or followed. Soon, my dog Smokie joined me, frantically happy to see me. I was thankful at that moment that he had not been noticeably hurt by Tony. I dropped to my knees and placed my head in his fur. He yelped softly, and I noticed a swollen area around his middle. He, too, had been hurt by that man. I let out gut-wrenching sobs in anger. Tony had no right to hurt anyone. Why was he like this? My poor dog couldn't even escape him. I dried my tears with my sleeve and got to my feet. I still needed to find Tim and kept hearing in my head that he was hurt and alone. It was that urgency that propelled me further. It seemed like it took me ages to get to that place.

When I stepped into the clearing, I scanned it for Tim. He was nowhere. I opened my mouth to yell his name but realized I did not have much of a voice from all the crying I had done in the last twenty-four hours. I croaked out his name as loud as possible, which didn't come much more than a whisper. Smokie perked his ears up and limped to one of the mounds on the other side of the clearing. At that moment, I became terrified of what I would find. How badly was he hurt, and would he need a doctor? How would I get him to a doctor if he needed one? Many questions rushed through my mind as I quietly walked across the clearing, ever aware that I had no cover. When I got to the other side of that mound, I was met by a scene that should not have been a part of my life. Tim had a swollen face with a black eye, a cut on his cheekbone, and bruises on his arm, and he clutched his side. I sunk slowly to my knees, tears running down my face.

"Tim?" I asked.

When he looked at me, there was so much pain in his eyes that it overwhelmed me. He let me raise his shirt to find a man's fist-sized bruise on his ribs.

The tears started again, and I felt his pain like it was my own. I didn't need to know what Tim did to cause this because I had felt it myself and knew it did not take much to turn Tony into a monster. He just stared at me through the pain, and all I could think was we needed to get away from all of this. We needed refuge and help. I opened my bag, found the alcohol wipes, and began trying to clean him up, placing band-aids where I could. Once that was done. I pulled out the clean clothes I had brought and helped him change. It was then I noticed that Tim did not have anything on his feet at all. I handed him the shoes I thought to grab and helped him slip them on.

I then laid one of the blankets down for him to lie on and covered him with the one I got from his room. I gave him a granola bar and a juice box. He thanked me but set them aside, snuggled under the blanket, and fell asleep. I cuddled up to him with the blanket I still had in my bag and slept beside him. Smokie stayed at our feet and kept watch. At that moment, all I could think of was that we needed to run away. There had to be a better way for kids like us to live. Tim slept for a long time after that.

I waited for Tim to wake up. When he finally sat up, I whispered,

"Tim, we need to get away from here. Tony destroyed the house and killed some of our pets. He'll do this again. We need a safe place to go."

He looked at me through swollen eyes and said,

"We can't leave Mom. She is in the same shape. She needs us to stay."

He, like me, was defeated in spirit and could not even fathom running away. We stayed out there for another day. Not once did either of them come looking for us. The next morning, Tim convinced me to go and at least look and see if Tony or anyone was at home. The thought of reentering that house made me sick to my stomach. I did not want to go back to the hurts and horrors that I would face once I entered that door. I did not want to suffer at the hands of people who said they loved me.

I did what my brother said, though. We got to the edge of the woods and looked at the house. From where we stood, we could only see Mom's truck. That encouraged Tim to walk towards the house. Mom must have seen us through the window and rushed out to hold Tim. She even engulfed me in a hug, and in that moment, I felt loved. It did not last long because I felt her go rigid and let me go. She helped Tim inside, crying the whole way, saying she was going to come looking for us. I saw the relief in Tim's eyes as Mom helped him inside. He glanced at me and with his eyes seemed to say everything was alright. I felt like an outsider at that moment, but I didn't know where else to go. Mom did not take Tim to the emergency room or hospital, but she did call a nurse friend to come and look at him. After she examined him, she told us that he had a bruised rib and did not need stitches on his face and that I had done a good job with the band-aids and pulling it back together.

Tony did not return for a few months after that. He would mail us his checks, and Mom spent the money how she saw fit, which meant we got a lot of animals over things that, as kids, we needed. She kept us home for a few weeks to allow Tim to heal. I don't know why she kept me home other than to keep me quiet about what had happened, not that I could bring myself to tell anyone. The rest of the school year was a blur, and I don't remember much. Grandma came and got us both for the summer, so we got a reprieve once again. I remember leaving that house wishing I would never see it again, and that part came true.

## **Pivot Point:**

This was an astoundingly hard period in my life, and then writing about it was painful to go back and relive. Unfortunately my life would continue to progress like this in the next few years. I realize this was graphic, but I want you to understand what happened in the presence of people who said they loved me. Also, no one at this time stepped in and tried to help us reach safety. As I look back, and maybe I'm just sensitive to it, you would think that neighbors, teachers, and people who saw us as children every day would have stopped and tried to help. As far as my knowledge goes, there was no help. I spent most days at home when I wasn't at school, and no one ever showed up. If my grandparents found out, they would never let on because they would always send us back to the same situation after a summer of refuge. Being the age I was in this era gave me a maturity that the adults around me did not possess. I was 8 when I fell off that horse and 10 when that tragedy with my brother happened. Unfortunately, that is not where the abuse stopped. It continued with Tony until he contracted cancer when I was 14. The abuse of my Mom is still there, but not as harmful physically. I continued to walk through that painful abuse from both of them until Tony passed away.

> *Don't be afraid, for I am with you. Don't be discouraged, for I am your God. I will strengthen you and help you. I will uphold you with my victorious right hand.*
> **Isaiah 41:10**

As I typed this, I found places where God led and directed me, even hiding me from harm. It wasn't happenstance that I felt urged to prepare for what would come. It wasn't a coincidence that the house's builders left a small unfinished hole for me to find. God also used visions of where Tim would be found to help me get to and help him. It was not God's plan that I would go through this time in my life, but he helped me through it. He did not send people to help us; I can't answer why. But I know I was instrumental in finding and helping my brother by listening to Him.

# CHAPTER 4

# Childhood age 11-14:

**AT THE AGE** of 11, we left that house and the horrors it witnessed. I was never so glad to leave the place where I witnessed such a harsh reality that was my home life. True to the course of our lives this far, everything was moved during our yearly visit to Grandma's. Mom and Tony had moved everything back to Missouri for my sixth-grade year in school. We moved into a small rural community in southeast Missouri, where everyone knew everyone's name and their business. This was unusual for us; we always lived in large communities and small cities when we moved. It was easier to fade into the background; everyone kept to themselves and left the tragedies in our home alone. It would be the same song and dance for Tim and me, new school, new people, and new worries.

By this point in my young life, I had succumbed to the fact that I would not have any steadiness in my life. We would constantly keep moving from one place to the next. I'm unsure of the reasons, but it has to do with not paying for the mortgage or rent, and my mom is known for writing bad checks. I would have to pull up every bit of courage I could muster to make it through one more year; that wouldn't matter because we would move again. I tried not to make any friends because I knew the heartache I would feel when I had to leave them. I entered the school year with that in mind. What I could not account for was how small that country school was going to be.

Everyone was so kind and went out of their way to care for me. I had grown familiar with being numb throughout the year just so I could survive the next.

I wasn't disrespectful, but I had created a protective wall around my fragile heart. I would not fall into the trap again and all people to be my friends and then lose them. Too much pain had occurred for me to be encouraged with that thought. When I walked into that 6th-grade class, I was astounded that there were only 13 other students. Instead of rows, all of the desks were in a U shape. I looked for the most secluded one, to find there wasn't any. I stepped in the door, and everyone came to greet me. This was something I had never experienced before.

In times past, I could slip in, and no one noticed, and I could fade into anonymity. They guided me to my new desk, and there, the teacher handed me a box of colored pencils and a pad of paper. The teacher looked right at me and said,

"You can use these to draw or color when you finish your work during the day."

I almost cried right then and there. I lost count of how often I was told I couldn't quietly draw, color, or even read when I finished my work. It was too distracting for everyone else.

"Can I read if I'm quiet as well?" I asked while looking at her.

"Certainly, as long as you can stay quiet." She spoke.

What type of school did I walk into? I looked around the room and, for the first time, realized how bright and colorful the room was. How the sunlight was allowed to shine into the room through the windows. Most of the classes I had been placed in before were cinder block and sterile, with little color and no room for creativity. This classroom encouraged that, and so did the teacher. At this point, I had not bothered to look at anyone directly in the face, but when I did, all I found was acceptance. My fragile shell was cracking, and my heart started to squeeze any little bit of hope it had. I swallowed that back down, though; I could not let them in. Losing friendships again would be too much; it would hurt too much. I resigned to the fact that even though I would be lonely, at least I would not be heartbroken. I thought to myself I would get through this year without letting anyone in. They wouldn't remember me after all when I moved next year.

Those negative thoughts would last for about a month before their weight would crumble before me. When it was recess or something that meant involvement from me, the other students would practically beg me to play with them. It was all I could do not to cave in. I needed these friends, but I could not risk the heartache, even if the pain of not giving in to their pleas was slowly killing me. I would sit on the swings until they slowly walked away to do their own thing. I could not explain why these kids wanted to let me play with them. Didn't they know that I would leave? No, of course not, because no one knew the pain I had gone through to get to this point in my life. It's not worth the time they put into me to be their friend.

I continued to believe the lies that I told myself. One day, on the way to recess, the teacher stopped me and told me to sit beside her desk. In times past, that meant I was in trouble. I usually stayed that way at other schools. After all, I would cause disruption in the classroom because I was bored. But I had yet to have that problem here; I could draw and read, and if one of the other students got distracted, they would be in trouble, not me. When she told me to go and wait for her by her desk, my stomach hit my shoes. I racked my brain at what I could have done to receive punishment and could not think of anything. I was near meltdown when the teacher returned to the room and closed the door. She must have noticed the fear I had on my face because when she looked at me, she smiled and said,

"You are not in trouble. I just wanted to talk with you," she said immediately.

She started the conversation with how well I was doing in her class. She said that my grades were fantastic. She appreciated that I stayed quiet in class. However, something was coming that I would not know how to answer. She looked at me, and it felt like she was staring into my soul. She asked in the most loving voice I had heard in a long time.

"I've noticed that you aren't making any friends. The other students want to get to know you. You don't talk or play with anyone. Why is that?" she stated.

I could not tolerate the pain any longer and started crying. This surprised her, and then I noticed compassion in her eyes. I wanted to tell her everything. I wanted to tell her the things that I had witnessed and how I had been abused. If she only knew a little of what I went through.

"I'll be moving at the end of the year like we always do. Why make friends?" I squeaked out before more tears came.

That's when she smiled at me and pulled me into a hug. She just held me and let me cry. She had to have known that there was more, but there was no way it would come out; it just couldn't. I cried out the hurt that I was feeling in her arms. Up until this point, no one held me and just let me cry. I was always alone and did not receive that love in my house. She gently pulled me back and handed me a tissue.

"Everyone needs friends, even if it is for a short while. Promise me that you will be brave and make friends. The other students in the classroom really want you to be friends with them." She said as she grabbed my face with her hands.

I knew what she was saying was true. However, opening up to that again was hard when my future was uncertain. It would have been so much easier if these kids did not like me, but they really did. She let me stay inside the rest of recess to get over crying. However, one girl returned inside before it was over and asked if she could grab her ball to play with outside. She turned and looked at me and must have seen that I had been crying. She immediately ran to me, asked what was wrong, and hugged me. I couldn't help but let a few more tears flow. She turned to the teacher and asked if it would be okay for me to go outside.

"Of course!" as the teacher nodded toward the door, the girl took me by the hand and led me to the playground.

All the kids in my class ran up to me and asked if I got in trouble or was okay. In truth, I was better than okay. I had people around me that cared, even if it would just be for a little while. I would have to open my heart up and let them in. The school pictures taken that year showed a very happy little girl in them. I had found a place to belong, even if it was just for a little while.

The house in this new place was different than we had before. We mostly lived in mobile homes and that one house that was built. This new house was built out of old wood that was recovered from the barn that used to be on the property. The house was two and half stories, and the whole house was unfinished from a remodel. Unfinished areas were found all over the house. The upper level was a loft that my brother claimed as his own. Because of the remodel, I no longer had an enclosed bedroom with a door. I had a bed in the corner as part of this large room upstairs. However, there was this little nook of an area that I could get to due to my size.

This area was small and had an opening to the laundry room below. I figured out that I could climb down from that place onto the top of the chest freezer and then quickly exit out the back door. It was vital for me to have a way to hide and be able to go out the door quickly. I never knew when the attitude would change in the house, so I ensured I had an escape route. My parents got the only enclosed area on that floor, and a door was quickly put there, but not one for me. I would have to make do with what I was given. I strung a rope across the opening of where my bed was and found some old sheets that weren't being used to hang up for privacy. This didn't do much to shield me from danger, but it was better than being in the open.

This new place was hard work for us. There was a fence to build, and the horses would need a barn before they came to live with us. My mom left the horses in Georgia with a friend who was boarding them. According to Mom, getting the horses here with us was paramount. We spent many days clearing, cutting the woods, and stringing fences in the field. As I looked across the field we were making, I didn't understand how this would be a proper pasture. It was nothing but rocks and bare dirt. There were a lot of weeds and very little grass. There would not be anything for them to eat. Forty acres were there; it was nothing but trees, rocks, and dirt. I kept going because I knew there would be consequences if I stopped and raised my concerns. It was back-breaking work, and I had many blisters and calluses by the time we got through. I had never experienced work like this before. This is also the first experience that I had with ticks and chiggers. I did not get very many ticks. Oh, but those nasty little bugs that are chiggers were on every part of my body. Even after taking a bath, I still felt them crawling on me, and the bites drove me to madness.

Tony soon noticed that my skin had scars, especially my legs, because of the bites and scratching them. He forced me to wear jeans all the time because he was not going to let anyone see me with those scars on my body. The problem was that I only had a few pairs of jeans because I had outgrown most of what I had. I asked Mom if I could get more and was told no. Tim had the brand name Levi's that Mom went out of her way to buy. I couldn't help but feel the sting of jealousy because he always got brand-new clothes, and I got thrift store finds. Not that it is a bad thing, but she would always get stuff from the seventies, and I didn't share her style, so to speak. I didn't get to go shopping with her either. Tim also had the loft where he could get away from everyone; he had new clothes and my mom's favor.

It was during this time that Tim grew an attitude with Mom. I used it as leverage to gain favor with Mom. She would argue with Tim and come outside to me, mad, and ask me not to be like that when I got his age. Not knowing what to do with this newfound attention, I promised her I would be good. If Tim got in trouble, I would share with Mom how good I was being right then. She started to pay attention to me more. Honestly, it felt foreign to me; I was not used to it. It grew into a relationship with her. One day, she even came to me and said that if Tony tried to touch me, I needed to tell her. I was blown away; I had prayed that something like this would happen for years. I don't know what has transpired between her and Tony, but he never touched me in that way again, even though he did try. I would just have to mention that I would tell Mom, and he would back off. I still ensured I was not in the house or hid if Mom was gone, just to be safe.

However, this extra attention would become a burden too. While I enjoyed it because I did not have it before, she would soon use it as leverage against me to watch my attitude and get extra work out of me or get something she wanted, which mostly happened. It became a game to her. I didn't know how the pieces worked; she did, and the rules constantly changed. As much as I craved her affection, I wish I had never started acting this way. I hated how she would act publicly with me, putting me on display everywhere we went. She would brag about my accomplishments or even something stupid that I had done. I wanted the attention, but it felt wrong or bad and forced.

Two of the biggest things that earned her attention were that I was good with animals and playing sports. I found that I had a natural gift with animals. I could feel their emotions and thoughts and read their body language. I could feel what they were going through

*;but God*

at that moment and could find a solution to help them. They often just needed soothing and assurance that it would be okay. It was funny how I was a natural at this when I barely felt it my entire life and had very few examples of it. I knew I carried no power, but I could empathize and understand their hurt, pain, and fear. Just being in my presence often was enough to calm them. Like they needed that from me. I often wished that I had someone in my life who had this same gift. I hope they can come into my situation and give me reassurance.

One time I remember specifically when my mom's favorite cat, Garfield, escaped outside. This cat had never been outside a day in his life. Mom was having a full-on freak out chasing this cat everywhere outside, and he was scared. There was no way he was about to come to a woman who was screaming at him. I still chuckle to this day, remembering the scene. We had an abandoned root cellar or storm shelter where Garfield ended up. Mom was scared to go near that place as if it was haunted. I don't know what she feared, but I never felt that. At this point, it started raining, and she became frantic. I was watching out the living room window and wondering how this would play out. That's when she turned around and saw me watching her. She ran back into the house and pleaded with me to go and save the cat. In my head, I thought, if he's in the storm shelter, he will be okay until the storm passes. She noticed my hesitation and told me that if I would go and get the cat, she would let me go to a friend's house I had been begging for. As much as I did not want to go out in the rain, being able to go to my friend's house sounded like heaven.

Getting away from here and treated normally was something I wanted badly. I let out an irritated breath, put on my rubber boots, slipped on my jacket, and trudged towards the storm shelter. The storm started to pick up, lightning struck everywhere, and the ground shook with the thunder. The rain was coming down so hard that I could barely see to walk down the hill towards the shelter. This was a place that, on a good day, would have been hard to get to without getting hurt because of the rocks everywhere and no dirt or grass to walk on. I got to the hill's edge and tried to see a way to get down it without falling. The one way we would always go down had a stream of water running through it, but that looked better than any other way. Hoping against hope that I would not fall, I took that first step.

The water was pouring down that hill so fast that it broke over the top of my boots several times. I could not see where to place my feet, so I would try to feel my way with each step. I had almost descended the hill until a rock rolled under my foot, and I lost my balance. The force of the water running down the hill pushed me over several rocks and cut up my legs. I wore shorts because I had that freedom when Tony wasn't home. When I was able to stand again, there was blood running everywhere down my legs. I was only a few feet from the shelter, so I carefully made my way over to it with each painful step. I stepped inside, where I was dry, and turned in the doorway, hoping to use the light to find where the blood was coming from. Both of my knees had gashes in them and were tender.

At this point, I no longer cared where the cat was. I was hurting and was stuck for the moment until the storm passed because the way up was worse than the way down. I decided to sit down and try to make the best of it, even though I was injured, wet, and cold. When I leaned back against the wall, out of the shadows came Garfield, purring like he had just had the best day of his life. I chuckled, remembering my mom chasing him in the yard in every direction.

Even though he was the reason I was in this mess, I couldn't blame him for wanting to escape that house because I wanted to escape, too. At that moment, I just started crying because my knees were hurting badly, and so was my heart. I longed for a sense of normalcy in my young life, where I didn't have to bargain with saving a cat to get to spend time with a friend. Where my accomplishments were not leveraged against me so that I could get the attention I wanted in return. To be freely loved like the cat loved me would be so wonderful. I stayed in self-pity until reality pulled me back. It had finally stopped raining. I waited a little longer until I was sure the water had stopped running down the hill. I wasn't sure that the inside of my jacket was drier than the outside, but I knew carrying the cat all zipped up inside would be safer. I shoved what I could of that large cat in my coat and zipped it up to the top. He didn't seem to mind, though, and he was purring. I looked down at my knees and noticed that the bleeding had stopped, but they were sore and stiff, and I knew I needed to get to the house and clean them up.

It wasn't easy going back up that hill. There seemed to be even more rocks than when I came down. I slipped several times and nearly lost the cat a few other, but I reached the top. With all the bending of my legs and slipping on the rocks, the bleeding started again. I rushed to the house and pushed open the door. Mom met me there and started yelling at me and asking why I took so long. I tried to explain, but she wouldn't hear it. She just yanked the cat from me and said I couldn't go to my friends now. All I could do was drop my head. Anger shot through my body, and I started shaking. I yelled that I didn't want to go anyway! I had never once yelled at anyone in that house, but I could not take it anymore.

I was tired of feeling like I was an afterthought. I was soaking wet, muddy, and bleeding, and not once did Mom take notice of my situation. Not once did she look at me and ask if I was okay. She marched up to me, slapped my face, and started calling me profanities I had heard about myself my entire life. For once, instead of cowering from that, I stood back up and stared at her. Willing her to do it again. I had been pushed too far that day. I braced for the impact that was sure to come. She raised her hand while clutching the cat, slowly lowering it, cursed some more, and then grounded me. She then marched off in a huff, mumbling under her breath.

I had no regrets yelling at her and gladly took the grounding. Even if my whole life was one of extensive grounding and confinement. I could not take any more on that day. I was shaking as I stomped into the bathroom to bathe and care for my wounds. No wounds were as big as the ones I felt in my heart. The tears slowly slipped down my cheeks as I undressed out of my all but ruined clothing. They had blood and mud soiled in them, and I had no idea how I would get that out. When undressed, I looked all over my body and noticed I had cuts and bruises everywhere. I hadn't even noticed until then how much everything hurt. I turned on the water for the bathtub, sat on the toilet, and sobbed silently, waiting for the tub to fill. I put a foot into the clear water, turning it reddish brown with the muck and blood that came off me. I slowly slipped into the water because my skin was set on fire by the temperature of the water on the cuts.

I screamed under my breath at the pain that shot through me. As I sat there, emotions and thoughts came over me. I started to pray that God would take me away from here or let me die. I did not know how much more I would be able to take. As I leaned back against the tub, this horrid thought came to my mind,

"What if you could just end it? What if you could drown in this bath water? No one would miss you; you could slip under the water, let your breath out, and slowly slip away; no one would notice."

That's what I did. I let all my air out and slipped under the water. My lungs and body started to burn. I tried to think about the people who would miss me if I did die. In my mind, no one would miss me. No one would listen or come and rescue me from this place. As I lay there, hoping the end would come swiftly, I heard a voice I could only describe as God's.

"Stop! Sit up now! There's more than this for you!" the voice thundered in my head.

The voice had a fatherly tone to it but not one of anger that made you scared enough to hide. No, this one had a loving authority: when it spoke, you felt loved. I needed that love so severely right at that moment. My world was so messy and hurtful. I did not feel love from earthly parents, but the love from the voice burned my heart but made it feel whole again.

I wished it would come back and surround me in a loving embrace I longed to feel. I sat in the bath water, coughing, trying to get air back in my lungs. I could not help but start sobbing while I sat in that dirty bath water. Once I cried myself out, I noticed just how dirty that water really was. I no longer wanted to sit in it.

I got out, drained the water, and cleaned out the dirt sitting on the bottom. Was the voice right? That someday I would leave all of this behind? Can I wash the dirt off my life and down the drain like in the bathtub? I looked down at my body and realized I wasn't fully clean yet. So I ensured all the dirt was gone, and the ring around the tub got washed down the drain. I plugged the tub back up and started filling it up again. When I got in this time, I only made the water a little dirty, and it stayed clean enough for me to get washed. I rushed through the bath to get out of the bathroom before someone else needed it. I didn't have any clothes to put on, so I dried myself as best I could and wrapped a towel around me. I looked at the cuts on my body and knew I would have to put bandages on some of them, especially my knees.

As I was bandaging my wounds, I realized that I shouldn't have tried to drown myself. I knew that I could not let them win. As bad as it hurt to be a part of this household if I killed myself, they would get what they wanted. A new confidence rose in me. I had to press on, no matter how hard it was to live here with them. Deep inside, I had the reassurance that there was more to life than this. I had to use two large pieces of gauze to cover my knees. They looked like I had fallen on a cheese grater. I finished by wrapping them with ace wraps. I cleaned up the paper mess, double-checked the bathtub for traces of dirt, and picked up my ruined clothing.

No one would ever know what I had attempted that day or how close I came to accomplishing it. I ensured the towel covered my body and quickly opened the door. Tim was right there staring at me in the face. I tried to push past him, but I didn't have an arm available to shove him. I didn't want to hear what he had to say. He was favored by Mom and could do no wrong. I stepped back in frustration.

"What do you want?" barely keeping my anger in check.

"What took you so long? That was stupid yelling at Mom like that." He boasted.

I rolled my eyes. I should have known Tim would have taken Mom's side.

"Tim, please let me go to my room, I'm grounded anyway." I pleaded.

He started again until he noticed all the bandages I had everywhere. A moment of compassion briefly entered his eyes, then returned to normal.

I wished he would remember how I helped him once and that he would help me right now. None of that was going to happen.

"Please, I want to get dressed, so let me out of this bathroom." I was growing angry.

Mom heard the commotion and peeked around the corner. Her eyes immediately went to me and looked at me up and down. Her face went from one of worry to a snarl.

"I just want out of the bathroom to go to my room, please," I spoke.

I knew my frustration came out in my voice, and I winced as I said it. She commanded Tim to step aside and then yelled that I would get another week for my attitude. I pushed past them and hurried to the stairs. Once past the landing, I heard them talking, so I quietly sat on the stairs underneath me.

"Why did she have all those bandages on her?" Mom asked.

"I think that she fell getting Garfield back for you. Didn't you notice that she left a muddy blood trail by the front door?" Tim responded.

"No, I was worried about the cat," she said while clutching Garfield.

When they went out of hearing distance, I got up and went to my room. This was the course of my life. It wasn't a surprise that my mom didn't check on me after that. I limped my way to my small corner of the upstairs. Looking around and listening to make certain I was alone, I got dressed. I was drained and partly hungry but didn't want to go downstairs to ask for food. I had a small stash of snacks and sodas, so I grabbed what looked appetizing and ate. I lay in bed and pulled the covers almost over my head. Doing this made me feel safe and comforted. As I drifted off to sleep, ideas began to form about my future and what it would look like. A small piece of my heart leaped with joy because I knew this would eventually be a memory.

Despite everything happening within my home's confines, I still grew in this new place. Before now, I was never allowed to be a part of anything requiring me to stay after school except when I was at Grandma's that one year. In my 6$^{th}$ grade year, I took a chance and asked Mom if I could play basketball. I almost didn't ask her because I was confident the answer would be no. She surprised me, though, and said yes. She got excited because she had played in high school and was on one of the first girls' high school teams in Pennsylvania. Those were her glory days, she told me.

I couldn't imagine my mom being athletic with how her body worked now. She was always hurting or unable to move or do anything. She said she would be at my practice to watch me and took me the next day to get some basketball shoes. Before I came to school here, I played basketball a little in P.E. I wasn't good at shooting, but

I could dribble the ball and play defense. I was nervous that first day of practice, even more so because my mom was watching and was the only parent there. I wasn't sure of my feelings right then.

On the one hand, I liked that she came and watched me, giving me attention; on the other, I knew there would be a catch, and she would be highly critical of me. We started some drills, and my hands were shaking so bad that I couldn't do anything right with them, not dribbling, not passing, and definitely not shooting. I could hear my mom yelling at me to do better with each mistake. She had no way of knowing that I could do better. She had never seen me play basketball before.

The coach allowed us a water break, and I went to the bathroom. As soon as the door closed, tears slipped down my face. I couldn't concentrate with her and the coach both yelling at me. I knew I could do better, and I wanted to. She just made me so nervous. One of my teammates walked in mid-cry and asked what was wrong. I told her I couldn't focus with Coach and my mom yelling at me. She then looked straight at me and said,

"Amanda, you can play ball; we play at recess. You are going to have to shut your ears to her. Here, wipe off your face and grab a drink; we need to get back out there."

When I returned to the court, I did the one thing I thought I would never do if my mom paid attention to me; I completely ignored her. When the coach talked, I only focused on him when he spoke, and the rest of the time, the ball and my teammates. Things started to turn around during that practice, and I slipped into my natural ability to play. I had a lot to learn, and it would take me the season to learn many skills. The coach worked hard with me during that practice. I learned to mimic his movements and remembered them as I moved through the drills. I had so much fun during practice; I felt free in a way I hadn't felt before.

Practice ended, and I went to the locker room to change. When I returned to the gym, my mom talked to the coach. As I approached the conversation, I could hear my mom's voice, and my stomach dropped. She used this voice on men to get her way, so I knew she was after something. Before I could ask what was happening, she told me to go and wait for her on the bleachers. I sat there for a few minutes before one of the other girls asked what my mom and coach were talking about. I just shrugged my shoulders. I couldn't think of one thing she would use that voice for right then. When they finished talking, she told me to come on, and we got in the truck to head home.

As I was waving goodbye to my friends, she exclaimed,

"Aren't you going to ask what that was about?"

I didn't want to know, but I knew I had to play along.

"What, Mom? What was it about?" I said in a monotone voice.

"You will find out next practice," she said as she smiled.

Her smile made me cringe. As much as I wanted to think maybe she was going to bring a snack or something, it would be something that gave her attention. I just sat there wondering what it could be. Our coach's daughter ran to me the following day when I got to school.

"Do you know what your mom asked my dad?" she asked.

"No, I don't," wondering what would come next.

Then she told me the thing that I dreaded hearing.

"Your mom had asked if she could be the assistant coach for the girls." She said.

Ugh, I knew it! I knew my mom would find a way to steal this from me. How was I going to ignore her now? When she would be in my face and yelling at me on the court? I almost gave up right then and wanted to be done before everything started.

I then looked at the girl and asked, "Can you talk to your Dad and see if he could put me with him to work one-on-one?"

She smiled and said, "He already thought of that. He thought his coaching would be better for you."

Great relief came over me. Under this coach, I soon developed good athletic skills and improved significantly over that short season. We won a lot of games, and when Mom was hugging everyone else, Coach always made sure to hug me after his daughter. I relished those moments because he saw my abilities and encouraged them. He would congratulate me as well when I worked hard. In that first season of basketball, I was known and had worth. That feeling is something I would carry for the next 6 years until I graduated high school.

That was also the only season my mom got to participate in the coaching process. The other coaches always shut her down. That didn't stop her from yelling at the coaches for not playing me the whole game, though. I was so embarrassed by that. I wished she would just let it be! With a few coaches I had, they let her influence their view of me. I loved the sport and enjoyed working hard for it. Sports at that school was the one thing that kept me going when times got rough.

Times did get rough, indeed. Tony did not come home much during this time. He still worked in Georgia and often wanted to avoid making the drive home. I remember one time that he was home, and he and Tim got into a physical argument again. This time, it was over sugar not being in the pantry. Mom needed to improve at keeping the house stocked with food. We didn't like it but weren't allowed to say anything, so we got by. When Tony was home, though, he expected it to be well stocked with all the money he had sent home. Tony would always ask what happened. She would lie about everything being so expensive or the kids eating everything. Of course, it was summer break, and we did need more than just breakfast and dinner.

The truth was all the animal stuff that she had purchased. Thousands of dollars had been spent to ensure the animals were well cared for. Because of that, we did not have much food and clothing ourselves. Surely, Tony saw past that and looked outside at the mess of animals we always had. One morning, Tony wanted to make sweet tea, and he couldn't find any sugar. We were home by ourselves with him again. He started yelling, and Tim was in the living room watching T.V. I was hiding in my room like I often was when Tony was home. I heard a scuffle start downstairs and knew Tim was getting beat again.

Tony screamed, "Why don't we have any sugar?"

I hurried out into the cubby from my room, where I could see Tony throwing Tim out the front door, yelling at him to go and get 10bs of sugar. I squeezed back into the corner of the cubby and prayed he wouldn't make it up the stairs. I would have to race out of the house through the back door from the opening in the laundry room. It was a 10ft drop, and I could get hurt. A bum leg would be better than being beaten by him. He started tearing up the house like the last time, but this time slower, and I could hear him wheezing like he was out of breath or couldn't breathe. Next, I hear silence. I strained with everything in me to hear where he was. Was he coming up the stairs? Did he pass out? What had happened?

I slowly made my way to the edge of the cubby and looked for him. I could see his head from the back because he had sat down and passed out on the sofa. That's where he stayed until Tim got back from the store. When Tim walked through the door, Tony woke up and started yelling again, but he didn't get up this time. Tony was upset that Tim had brought home 2–5-pound bags of sugar instead of 1–10-pound bag. Tim did some yelling of his own, said they didn't have anything other than 5-pound bags and skirted past Tony to put the sugar away. I could then hear Tim making his way to the stairs and quietly moved back into my room to meet him at the top of the stairs. What I saw was like looking at a picture from the past. His face was black, blue, and swollen again. However, I saw pure anger instead of sorrow and hurt this time. His face finally displayed what I had felt so many times in this family.

He looked at me and said, "I'm leaving for a few days, and you should, too. I'm going to a friend's house and will be back when he leaves."

Tears slipped down my face. I had no friends I could get to or know where they lived. I wasn't allowed to go anywhere. I went and packed a small bag to be able to get out of the house, at least until Mom got home.

I wasn't safe with Tony here. Tim left before I could follow him to see where he went. I went to the edge of the cubby again and slowly lowered myself onto the freezer, praying that Tony would stay on the sofa and not hear me. Fortunately, I heard him in the bathroom and knew I needed to quickly reach the back door. I was almost to it when he heard me. There was no way that I would stay there in that house. My hands shook as I twisted the knob. I went through the door and saw him rounding the corner in the laundry room as I closed it. He was already yelling at me to come back into the house. I couldn't face him. If I stayed in the house, I would look like Tim before long. I sprinted to the woods behind the house and was hidden before he got outside the door. From where I hid behind a large tree, I could hear his ragged breath across the yard. I peeked around the tree so that I could see him. He went into a coughing fit so violently that he dropped to his knees and started crying for help. I could make out blood on his shirt from the coughing.

My compassionate side said that I needed to go and help him. I felt terrible for him, but I knew if I went back as soon as he got his hands on me, he would start smacking me around. So, I just stood there watching him from the woods. He eventually got propped up by the house, and his breathing slowed down. To see this sick, twisted man who would rattle the house with his anger, to be so weak, was considerably out of character. I slipped further into the woods when I noticed his head fall back against the house. I still didn't know where I was going. However, returning to the house was not an option.

So further into the woods, I went. I found a large, downed oak tree and cleared an area next to it. I sat down and leaned up against it. I let my head fall back, and my imagination started to flow. I longed for someone to hold me and make the harsh reality disappear. I imagined a home with warmth and food could be found in the cabinets. I saw in that vision that I had clothes that fit and weren't threadbare. I felt the sting of loneliness in that moment and longed for a home that loved me. I was tired of constantly guessing and watching everyone's mood and movements. I curled my knees up to my chest, wrapped my arms around them, and let the tears flow. I almost broke in that moment and succumbed to the reality that this was my life. That my life would always be this way. There was such a fight in my mind that I needed to let go and give up. This voice, though, came softly and said something my heart longed to hear.

"You will have that and more; don't give up. I have a plan and a purpose for you. I am sending someone who will love you despite this and help you heal," the voice echoed softly.

What was trying to break me in that moment left and the feelings of doubt with it. I felt renewed in that moment. Even though looking around me, nothing had changed, I knew it would someday. My stomach growled, reminding me I didn't bring any food or drink. I needed to get back in the house, but I didn't know how that would happen. It was getting dark, and I did not have anything to protect me from the cold of the night.

It was not going to be an easy feat to get back in the house. I got to the edge of the woods as it was almost dark. If no lights were on in the house, that would make finding Tony more difficult. Worse yet, if he was sitting in the dark, he would be able to see me if I peered in. I was almost safer outside with the cold and wild animals than I would be in that house. My stomach growled again, reminding me it had been a long time since I had any food. My shoulders slumped; I would have to get inside, even if it was just to grab food and drink. The house had no lights on, so I would have to do my best to avoid getting spotted.

I went around the house, sticking close to the siding so I wouldn't be seen. Every window I looked in, I didn't see him. I approached the back door and opened it slowly, praying it wouldn't squeak. I stepped inside and cautiously closed the door until the lock touched the door frame. I stood in darkness, waiting for movement or something telling me where he was. I heard a movement upstairs and knew he was in their bedroom. I breathed a sigh of relief, but fear was on the edge of it. Going upstairs wasn't an option. Ideas, I needed them! Hunger wasn't going to let me go back outside. I was five feet from the kitchen. I slowly looked around for something I could shove into the bag that I carried on my back. I found a bag of chips and two cans of Vienna sausages. I grabbed those and put them into the bag. I looked around and found a banana on the counter. I then stepped cautiously over to the fridge and quietly opened it. There was a small piece of cheese and a soda in there. Everything went into the bag. I wanted more in case I got hungry later, but there was little that I could grab and take with me. I scanned the fridge for anything else to help, but nothing was there.

Exhaling in frustration, I closed the door. I stopped for a moment and listened; all movement had stopped. Tony hadn't come downstairs, so he must have fallen asleep. I wasn't going to chance going upstairs and getting caught by him. I looked around and saw a blanket on the sofa. I tiptoed over to it. As I put my hand out to grab it, I noticed Mom's candy stash. It was a bag filled with chocolate, licorice, and gummies. I knew it was a bad idea, but I swiped it off the side table she had it on. She always had a stash of candy that she kept from us. We could be starving, but you still could not touch it. She would be angry, but I didn't have much food in my bag. I pushed the blanket in the bag after the candy stash and zipped it up. Now, I needed a light to help me see in the darkness. I looked around by the back door and found our lantern and my nasty farm coat. It would be better than nothing, so I slipped it on. I looked down at my legs and feet, hoping that what I had on would keep me warm. I slipped out the door and closed it quietly.

As soon as I slipped off that back step, I realized I still had no place to go other than the woods, which was not appealing. We had coyotes, mountain lions, and bobcats in our woods, and I didn't want to come face-to-face with one. I could go to the barn. It would be shelter and I would be safe from the elements. It wasn't huge, but the horses could come and go from the stalls. There was hay in there and their tack. It was a shelter for me. So that's where I went. I would have to sneak around the edge of the fence. If I went to the front of the house, Tony could see me through their upstairs window. I would have to go around the back of the house and sneak to the fence. I went around the outside edge of the fence until I was on the side of the barn that couldn't be seen from the house. From there, I could quickly sneak in the front door. Once in the barn, I felt safe and took a much-needed breath. We didn't have electricity in the barn, so I switched on the lantern and placed it on a hay bale. That created enough light for me to see everything in there. I needed to make a place for me to sleep. I could feel exhaustion in my limbs from the fear of the day. I got two old saddle pads, opened them, and stacked them on the dirt floor. Then I stacked the square hay bales up in twos to keep the air off me; hopefully, I would stay warm. I sat down on the edge of the bales and pulled the blanket out of the bag with all the food and the book I always had in there. I needed to eat and wanted something warm and comforting, but there was no chance of that. I ate what I had and was thankful my stomach would get food. Sitting there eating my meager meal, I looked around the barn and noticed how nice everything was. The tack we had gleamed in the dim light with bright shiny buckles. I smelled the rich leather and horse scent. I loved the way both of those smelled. I could not enjoy it, though, because it was a grim reality to be in the midst of. If only I was cared for like these saddles and horses. They had bags of expensive feed and clover hay to eat, the best of everything. And here I sat with Vienna sausages and chips to eat for a meal because my house was too harmful to enter. One of the horses we had at the time stepped into the light and softly neighed at me. It was as if she could feel the pain of the situation. She moved her head up and down, asking me to come to her. I stood up and walked toward her. She reached out her beautiful neck, stretching to get closer to me. I opened her door and stepped in. That's when she wrapped her neck around me and pulled my small frame up against hers. In times past, I was the one who calmed her; now, she repaid the favor.

She knew at that moment I needed love. That unraveled my tightly wound resolve, and I let out horribly loud sobs that seemed to shake the whole barn. This horse understood the love that I needed better than my parents. The more I cried, the more she pushed me into her side. I cried until I couldn't squeeze out another tear, and I was dry and weak from the release. I was tired of pushing everything down and trying to carry on like nothing happened. I was exhausted from being told I needed to shove everything aside and get over it. I was over being pushed aside and told I was stupid and worthless. I felt loved with her neck wrapped around me. Sadly, a horse sensed my sorrow and hurt, not another human. I was fatigued, so I squeezed the horse's neck again and stepped out of the stall. I needed sleep. I cleaned up the mess I had made, shoved the rest of the food into my bag, and crawled over the bales into my makeshift pallet. I pulled the blanket over me and prayed that I would be safe in the night ahead.

Surprisingly, I had a very peaceful sleep and was waking up when Mom opened the door to the barn. A look of surprise and then anger crossed her face at seeing me in the barn.

"What the hell are you doing in here? Why would you sleep in the barn? Get back to the house, I need help with chores, and I need you to start in the house." She yelled.

She barely took a breath in between and never long enough for me to answer anything. She had to have known, or did she not even care. I dreaded going back into that house! I did not want to see Tony and get smacked around because I escaped him yesterday. I felt sick with dread, but I gathered my stuff and went to the house. When I approached the house, I noticed Tony's truck was gone. Relief washed over me! At least I could clean the house in peace. I wondered if Mom knew that Tim was gone. Not that I could tell her anything because Tim didn't say what friend. I took my stuff upstairs and changed out of yesterday's clothes. Any remnant of that peaceful sleep was now gone and, thankfully, yesterday's troubles. My mind went to the day I would no longer have to endure this. I couldn't stay there long before reality came rushing back.

I went downstairs and started cleaning before Mom returned from doing animal chores. Mom had to work today, too, so I would be home alone. I had this quiet happiness stirring in me as I cleaned. Mom came in, saw that I was cleaning, and went about getting ready for work. She said I didn't need to worry about doing evening chores because she would be back before then, and we were out of feed. I asked her to get some food at the grocery store, and her response was she would see, which usually meant no. I shrugged my shoulders and went back to work. She wouldn't ruin this mood of freedom I would have for a few hours. I would cherish this time alone. I wouldn't have someone watching my every move or telling me I couldn't do something or wasn't doing it right. I still had the dishes left before I could have a short time of freedom. Mom went quickly out the door, reminding me she would need help feeding when she came home. Once finished with chores, I planned to go outside and brush out the horse that hugged me last night. However, it started to get cloudy outside, predicting rain was about to start; the clouds were dark and menacing. While staring out the window, I filled the sink with my hands in the water.

I remember seeing a blinding bright light outside, and then I remember waking up on the floor. Man, my head and back hurt, and my legs were weak. What had happened? I felt the need to lay down, but I looked at the sink, and the dishes were still dirty. I looked at the kitchen wall clock and noticed it was getting close to time for Mom to be home. What happened to my short time of freedom? I put my hands in the water; it was ice cold. Then, a connection was made in my memory. I remembered a bright flash just before I woke up from the floor. The storm must have had lightning in it. It struck close to the house and must have gone through the metal pipes and into the dishwater. I did a once-over of my body. The only thing that felt off, besides my head and back, was that my hands tingled and were red. I tried as fast as I could to get the dishes done.

I really needed to lie down and hopefully get rid of this headache. I slowly dragged my feet up the stairs to my corner and fell into bed. The next thing I knew, I was being shaken awake by my mom, who was furious with me. Everything was foggy and muddled in my brain, and I couldn't comprehend why she was in my room freaking out. Her voice sounded like the teacher from Charlie Brown. I couldn't focus on what she was saying. She kept yelling at me to get out of bed and help her, but I couldn't get my legs or arms to respond. When I went to push myself up with my hands, pain seared through them, and I cried out. She finally stopped her tirade to take note of the situation and then started on another round of yelling, asking if I had taken any drugs or alcohol. I remember getting struck by lightning.

"I got hit by lightning!" I said, barely loud enough for her to hear.

Worry came across her facial features for a second and then turned to anger again. I had had enough in the middle of all her accusations and how I got hit.

I looked at her, and with my bit of strength, I yelled, "Dishes, I got struck doing dishes!" and passed back out.

As I passed back out, I realized I didn't care anymore. The last couple of days had been horrendous, and I needed rest and to take care of myself. Waiting for Mom to take care of me wasn't going to happen. She didn't take me to the hospital when I fell off that horse all those years ago, and she wasn't going to do the right thing now. I lay there with my eyes closed and faded into darkness, not hearing what else she was saying, nor did I care.

Tim finally returned home after a few days, and I got over feeling like my body was on fire after the lightning strike. To this day, I still don't know if Mom realized he had gone to a friend's house. When he returned, however, he looked better compared to when this had happened before. Tony returned in a few days. I was forced to sit at his feet like I used to because I had run away from him. He kept asking me to smile pretty for him. Every time I looked at him, I noticed his eyes were cloudy and his breath short. The color of his face was off as well. I knew that he did not feel good. I sat there in worry and waited until Mom came through the door from evening chores. She glared at me as she passed, but it had no effect.

I couldn't help the situation any more than she could. I politely asked Tony if I could get up and get a drink from the kitchen. He allowed me to move, but only if I brought him a beer back. I stood up and followed Mom to the kitchen, where I quietly tried to get her attention. At first, she tried to ignore me until I blocked her way out of the kitchen. She told me to get out of her way under her breath. In passing, I managed to ask her to look at Tony; something was wrong with him. When she nodded, I stepped back and grabbed a beer from the refrigerator. As I entered the living room, I noticed Mom standing over Tony and having difficulty getting him to talk to her. She looked at me worried. She still cared for him. I could see it on her face. I never understood why she still loved him, with as much pain as he put us through in this part of our lives. I went to help stand him up, and he had little weight. He was supposed to be this large man, and there wasn't anything left of him.

What was wrong with him? I would have to help Mom get him into the car. We did not have an ambulance service where we lived. Tony must go to the nearest Army hospital, Fort Leonard Wood. This way, It was faster than waiting for someone to respond here with the ambulance, which would take an hour. Tony didn't have that long. As soon as we got him in the car and I closed his door, Mom raced away, spitting rocks in her wake. My gut told me it wasn't good, and I wondered if he would ever return home.

After three days, we waited to hear back from Mom. She did not call to let us know what had happened while she was gone. Tim did not seem to mind that something was wrong with Tony. I couldn't blame him; life hadn't been easy for us, to say the least. He had graduated high school and would go to college soon, leaving all of this behind. My mind, however, went a different way. If Tony died, then that meant that we would lose his income. What would happen to us then? Would we have to move? There were so many unknowns, making my stomach sick to think of it. For three days, I waited to learn the outcome. Life had to carry on, though; the house was kept clean, and animals were fed, and there were so many of them. I was doing chores and walking back to the house when I heard the crunch of gravel. I looked up and saw Mom's car coming down the driveway. I raced toward it and noticed only one person in the front. My stomach felt sick. Trying to calm my nerves, I told myself I was jumping to conclusions. Mom came to a stop and jumped out. Her body language said to me that she was distressed.

"Help me unload, there's a lot." She yelled.

I looked, and she had several bags of groceries in the back seat, and the trunk was loaded down with feed for the animals. This was a lot to be for the week. But I listened to what she wanted, carried the groceries inside, and then put the feed in the barn.

This was more food than we had in a long time, and it didn't make sense. Where did all the money come from for this? While I was unloading everything, I overheard Mom telling Tim that Tony was in critical condition and had a large mass in his airway. The hospital would be transporting him to Denver for cancer treatment in the next few days, and she would be going with him. They would be gone for a month or two and should be back before the end of July. She would talk to the neighbors and see if they could check in on us to see if we were okay. We had several people nearby, but Mom didn't have a great relationship with any of them. I couldn't see how that was going to help anything. I hoped that they would be kind enough to stop by and check on us. It took me a while to unload everything and put it away, mainly because Mom didn't help, and there was much to put away.

Mom raced around the house, gathering everything she needed for her and Tony. When I finished everything, I needed to sit just for a moment. Unloading all that was tiring, and my thirteen-year-old body was tired from caring for everything the last few days. I was not in the kitchen for longer than a minute when she started yelling that I was lazy and needed to make sure that everything was taken care of. What? In my mind, I knew better, but I couldn't help what came out of my mouth. I said,

*Childhood age 11-14:*

"Can I please sit for a minute after taking care of everything the last few days and then unloading most of the car by myself."

Was she blind? I spent over an hour unloading the car and putting everything away while she and Tim talked. Not once did she say two words to me or notice the multiple trips I made back and forth while she sat. I didn't say anything about helping me because I figured she was tired and needed a break and a moment to figure things out.

I almost missed her raising her hand to hit me, but I saw it out of the corner of my eye. I dodged most of it except for her fingertips catching my cheek. The action made me bite the inside of my mouth, and I tasted blood. Because I moved back, she lost her balance and fell on me. Both of us hit the top of the table. When we hit, I shoved her off and stepped away. Somehow, in all of that, she got hurt and started crying. She held her wrist and whined like a wounded animal. I stood looking at her, not really knowing what to do. I knew not to comfort her because that would end up worse. I couldn't leave because I felt terrible about that happening. Third, I wondered in the back of my mind if she was hurt. Her hands hit my chest when we fell, and I pushed her straight up to a standing position. I had a strong feeling that it was the third. So, I stupidly called her out on it.

"How did you get hurt? You fell on me, not the table." I ask with more calm than I felt.

Yep, that did it, I hit the button. She went from this wounded animal to cussing in fury. She started swinging her hands at me. Missing each time until I got backed into a corner, and she finally landed one across my face. It was hard enough to make my lip bleed. I couldn't tolerate it anymore. I caught the next hand and squeezed. I was strong for 13; the manual labor I did all the time helped with that.

"Stop hitting me!" came out of my mouth before I knew what happened. I was so tired of it all.

When I raised my eyes to her face, she had this look of fearful surprise. I just wanted to rest for a few minutes! How did we get here? I know that it wasn't wise to say what I said. What about treating me like a slave all the time when you and Tim don't do much. I dropped her hand, gritted my teeth, and said,

"I am going to my room."

I grabbed the food I had set aside as a snack and marched toward the stairs. All the time, Mom was on my heels, screaming curses at me. But they were drowned out by the anger I felt inside. Once past the landing, I let the tears flow. I hated this, all of it! Nothing I said or did would be good enough for her. I want to say that I grew tired of trying to please her, but I didn't. I desperately wanted her to love me and would continue trying to get that for much of my life.

They were gone for two and a half months, and I had a love-hate relationship with this time. Loved it because I didn't have to worry about the abuse if I didn't do something right away, and I didn't necessarily have to keep a schedule. I was not too fond of it because I did most of everything. Tim had a job or often went to a friend's house. When he was home, he either slept or sat watching T.V., a luxury we didn't have before. I would ask him to help, but I was always put off. I learned how to cook during this time as well. Mom would never let me in the kitchen while she was cooking. Tony always said that if I could read, I could do almost anything, and I took that to heart. We had a couple of cookbooks in the kitchen, and when I got hungry, I would open them up and learn. I learned what tasted good and what didn't. I learned to cook raw chicken and beef. I loved cooking, and it gave me a sense of purpose. I did most of my cooking when Tim wasn't there and made extra special meals. My favorite was baked chicken, boxed mashed potatoes, and green beans. It doesn't sound like much, but to me, it was heaven. Especially when all I would usually get was meals of convenience. Mom didn't cook full-blown meals very often, so this was great. I also did all the house and animal chores.

Tim didn't like the animals and said we didn't need that many. We still had them, though, and they needed to be taken care of. I learned a system of working smarter, not harder, with the animals so that I could get done quickly. The way Mom always wanted it done took a long time. I also gained independence during this time and learned I was intelligent despite being called stupid regularly. I would wake early to beat the heat and finish the house before breakfast. Then I had the rest of the day until close to evening when I fed the animals again. Deep inside, I wished everything could stay this way, but I knew my time of freedom would be short-lived. Mom called once a week. While I talked to her some, she mostly wanted to talk to Tim. I only got a little information from Tim on how things were going with Tony. He would only get off the phone and say he was still alive. We were still waiting for a date when they would be home. I anxiously waited for the news that they would be home every day.

The day finally came. I almost finished cleaning the house and heard gravel crunch outside. When I peered out of the window, I finally got my answer. Anxiety hit the pit of my stomach. They were home. I should have been happy, but dread descended over me. What new challenges would I face with Tony being sick? I reluctantly went outside and asked if help was needed. If I didn't, I would hear about it. I stepped outside, and Mom was fussing over Tony, helping him get out of the car. He was a shell of the man I remember before this happened. His face was different; it had a light to it, and his eyes were clear. The skin on his face was gray and shallow, but his eyes shone with joy? I couldn't put my finger on it. It drew me to him. I was hesitant to walk closer. Our eyes met, and I saw sorrow and regret enter them, and tears poured down his face. He reached for me, but Mom slipped a cane into his extended hand, and he was pulled away by her.

He was unsteady on his legs, and I could tell he had very little energy. He glanced back over his shoulder while Mom moved him forward. I wanted to follow, but Mom barked at me to get the car unloaded. Responsibility moved me back to the car, and I began to unload. Life would return to normal, and I would lose my freedom. As I walked through the door carrying luggage from the car, I saw Mom crying and giving Tim a long hug. A pang of jealousy ripped through me. She was telling him how good of a job he did on everything, and Tim didn't even stop to correct her.

"Are you kidding me? I did everything! I busted my butt every day so that the animals would be taken care of and the house would stay clean!" I said under my breath.

Hot tears rushed to my eyes, and I took everything I was carrying upstairs to their room. I had not cried once while they were gone. I set everything down in their room and quietly rushed to mine. I dropped to my knees beside my bed and sobbed. Any confidence that I had built in myself was wiped away all in an instant. It was right then that a resolve built in me. As soon as I graduated from school, I would be gone. Working that hard taught me that I could make it independently. However, any thoughts or plans I had were interrupted by Mom yelling at me to finish unloading the car.

As I came downstairs, I glanced at Tony on the sofa. He had his head tilted back on the couch. I stepped in his direction, but Mom angrily gestured for me to finish unloading the car. I took one more glance and went outside. When I got everything unloaded, I quietly went to my room and stayed. It was hot this time of day upstairs in the summer, and I had got used to the cooler downstairs. I didn't feel like I could be in the room with them and be able to sit. Undoubtedly, Mom would have something for me to do. I turned on my little fan and grabbed a book to read. Being in my warm room made me sleepy. I didn't intend to fall asleep, but it happened. The next thing I realized

Childhood age 11-14:

was that Mom was standing over my bed, shaking me and wanting me to get up. I didn't understand why she was bothering me. She was saying something about going to take care of the animals. I looked up at the window in my room; it was bright outside, meaning it was hot.

"They will be fine until the sun goes down a little." I sleepily said.

In my sleepy state, I didn't realize what I said. I felt a hard smack upside of my head, and it made me bite my lip. I immediately sat up and had a mixture of anger and fear coursing through my body. I had gone close to three months without anyone doing anything like that to me. I erred on the side of stupidity and repeated the same thing.

"They will be fine, and I will wait until it's a little cooler," I said, holding back my anger.

I could tell she was angry, and her anger came around again, and this time, I caught it. I was tall enough to look my mom in the eyes. The air cracked with anger between us. She was about to swing again when Tim called for her, and her attention got divided.

Before she left, "You will be taking care of the animals!" she said through clenched teeth.

I almost said, "When I feel like it!" but I thought better of it and let it go.

She stormed out of my room, and I could hear her talking to Tim about me on their way down the stairs. I put my face in my pillow and screamed. I had tried hard to ensure everything ran smoothly without her and Tony. I don't know what I expected, but it wasn't this. I thought I would receive recognition, a pat on the back, a thank you, but not this.

The hot tears came again. I wiped them away with my hand. I slipped on my shoes because Mom wouldn't leave me alone until she got what she wanted. So out into the hot air, I went. Just as I predicted, everyone was okay. I gave them their evening meal and filled their waterers anyway. I went through the motions of this, but inside,

I felt so much anger towards her. I should never have been left alone because now I longed for the freedom I had lost that morning. I knew it would be long before I saw it again.

From August to January was a time of great trial for our family. We lost Tony's income, but nothing changed with that. Mom always spent it frivolously anyway. Tim went to college and only made a few trips home. Mom was gone most of the time with work. For some reason, she thought it was a great time to return to college to study nursing. Which made everything fall on my shoulders, even the care of Tony. I would wake up early, feed and water the animals, go into the house and clean a little, and then make sure Tony had everything he needed for the day. I would have to help him clean up his throw-up because of the chemo treatments. I would also make sure that he had his walker close to him. I would tell him about my schedule for the day, and he would nod and fall asleep before I left. He didn't like being helped and was adamant that he would be okay. I was still playing sports and would have a friend bring me home.

I would briefly stop in the house to check on him and then go outside to take care of the animals for the evening. I noticed his attitude had changed, and I wasn't afraid of him. One evening, after chores, I came inside to find him cooking, and he was happy. He asked me to go wash up and help him set the table. Everything about this man had changed, and I was drawn to it. I did as he asked. Dinner was meager. Canned chicken soup and bologna sandwiches, but I was grateful. Most nights, I had to find something that would work for both of us. We sat down at the table, just the two of us. I wanted to be wary of the situation but couldn't leave.

I started to pick up my spoon, and Tony stopped me. "Please, can I say grace?" He asked.

I slowly nodded my head and then bowed it. I listened to his awkward prayer to God and took comfort in it. When he was done, our eyes met, and I saw tears in his.

Before I could look back at my food, he said, "Sorry…… I am so sorry for how I treated you. I should have never done what I had done to you. Please, I hope one day you can forgive me. I am so proud of you and your hard work making sure everything gets done. You don't complain and take responsibility for things you shouldn't have to. I hope someday, someone sees what type of person you are. I also hope your mom treats you better than she does now."

With tears streaming down my face, I could only shake my head to acknowledge him. He then asked if I had heard of someone called Jesus. I shook my head again, too overcome with emotions to speak. He then asked if he could share his story with me? Again, I nodded. There was a chaplain in the hospital who would visit him daily. He had told him over and over that he didn't want to know Jesus and that he had done too many things to change where he was going. One night, after a challenging procedure, he had taken a turn for the worse and flat-lined. He was considered dead.

Tony didn't go into detail, but what he saw scared him. When he finally recovered from that and woke up, the chaplain was the first person he wanted to see. The chaplain came to his room, and they talked. He showed him how to know Jesus by being saved. That explained the light in his eyes when he got home, the change in behavior and attitude, and why I could be around him without fear. I had felt what it was like to be saved, too, and there is nothing like it. He then looked at me and said he could tell I was also saved because of how my eyes looked; they were clear and sparkling. A smile came to my face, and he smiled too.

He then looked at me and said, "I love when you smile. That smile when you were little would help me. Like a little ray of sunshine.

Your smile would break through the cloud in my head and make me feel better."

He then started to weep, begging me to forgive him. After that, I did something I rarely did without prompting. I got up and hugged him. We wept on each other's shoulders. This was the first time I felt actual love from this man. Fear was nowhere to be felt. He released me and said I needed to eat. We ate in companionable silence, and I cleared the table when we were done. I wish I could say that Tony got better from cancer, but I can't. The following week, Tony's health took a turn. He became bedridden and needed more time than I could handle with going to school. Mom had to nursing school, so that she would be home more with him. I watched Tony deteriorate even further to the point that he could barely get up or even eat. He was still with us for Christmas that year, and gift-giving was sparse.

I had 10 dollars that I had saved, and I bought a magnetic racing track set and some candy for all of us. Come Christmas morning, I presented my gift to the family. Tim, Tony, and I put it together on Tony's bed. We played with it for hours, laughing. Mom kept to herself on the sofa reading, never joining in. We didn't have a Christmas dinner or anything like that, but it is one of the fondest memories I have of Christmas because, for once, there was a sense of joy in the house that I had never felt. Tony passed away less than a month later. It was gut-wrenching to watch him fade to nothing. I learned to pray during this time and begged God not to take this man who made me feel loved. I know it was selfish, but if he died, who would love me then? I had a genuine fear of what my future would look like.

**Pivot Point:**

So much happened in this chapter. We stopped moving as a family and finally stayed put. This was a great help to my self-esteem as a young teenager. Life was still hard, but I seemed stronger and more intelligent than I was given credit for. The abuse was still prevalent, but not from Tony as much as my mom. Even though my mother took glory in it, I was allowed to play sports.

> *"And we know that in all things God works for the good of those who love Him, who have been called according to His purpose."* **Romans 8:28**

During Tony's cancer treatments, I gained a sense of independence and learned that despite everything wrong that I had heard about myself, it was untrue. I am sorry that it took Tony to get cancer before he was saved. Looking back, I believe God was at work in that circumstance. I am very grateful that I got to share those last few months with a changed man and feel love from him. Tony's testimony started me on my path to wanting to know God for myself. We never know how long a situation will take or how long you will have it. Looking back, I can see God's hand in that situation and know that even though all that happened to me and our family, He was still good through all of it. So, no matter what happens, God is still good, and He is still working.

# CHAPTER 5

# Childhood 14-18: High School

**THE REST OF** my eighth-grade year was rough. I didn't know how to deal with the sorrow I felt from Tony dying. Mom would ridicule me for crying over him. This was yet another thing that I would have to push down. I didn't know how much more I could push down. Within a few months of Tony dying and just long enough for Mom to receive Social Security checks, Mom had found another man named Sam. It didn't take long for her to start spending much time at his house. This left me to take care of the house we lived in since coming to Missouri. It wasn't long until we were gone from that house, too. Mom had stopped making the payments after Tony's death, and we were being evicted.

I was worried that the next man she had found would be like Tony because it seemed her man picker was broken. He wasn't like Tony, but he wasn't great either. He was a know-it-all and not one I could talk about God to. He didn't seem to care for either me or God. We tolerated each other. I had a room all to myself, which was good. It was the whole second floor, and I had 2 ways to go in and out. There was a set of stairs to be lowered by pulling them down inside. I could also go out the upstairs door with a porch outside. I no longer worried about an escape route, but I had one just in case.

This guy liked his women wearing a lot of makeup, and I would secretly laugh when Mom put makeup on. She looked like a clown with dark blush and bright blue eye shadow. He would also make fun of her when she had it on. He even convinced her to cut all her hair into a pixie cut. I pitied her sometimes; she tried so hard to fit the mold of what this man wanted. She got to keep her animals and had lots of land to have more; it must have been worth the sacrifice to her. I had no choice but to be there.

Mom's mood seemed to darken even more toward me during this time. She became highly critical and would often make fun of me. She also started smacking me in the face or head a lot, which drove me to anger. Again, I became the workhorse that I had always been. We had a menagerie of animals, from snakes to lizards, exotic birds, deer, llamas, and the regular farm stuff we had always had. It seemed she was always buying more and more. She didn't have to work now, so most of her time and money was spent with them. She started taking me to horse shows, and I was allowed to compete. I loved the horses and spent many hours training them. I was still playing sports and would sign up for anything that would keep me away from that house. Mom didn't like all my running around, but she would revel in the glory I brought her.

I wanted more of a relationship with her, but that would never happen in this time. We shared a few rare moments of open-hearted conversation, but it would be used against me later. I couldn't help myself in those moments because it seemed she cared for me, and I needed an outlet. Life was better here, but not by much. At least I didn't have to fear what this man would do to me. He didn't have much gumption and would rather talk and criticize me. I would brush off most of it, even though sometimes his words hit their mark.

I still played sports during this time because it kept me sane. It gave me a sense of freedom and that I could do anything I put my mind to. I played basketball because it was my mom's crown, but I learned to love it. It was an escape because this was a constant no matter what I was going through. No matter how much competition I faced on that court, I played, strategized, and countered my opponent's every move. Playing time was just for me. I was picked to be out there because I was dependable and could handle what was thrown at me. I could have improved at outside shots, but I excelled at rebounds. I loved to exploit my opponents' weaknesses, and finding them became a challenge to me. The more I played, the more I could block out my mother's voice, yelling at everything I did wrong. The more I played, the more the world started to make sense. This was a constant to me when everything in my world was always changing, and nothing was ever trustworthy. My world was in constant chaos. This was my calm. I needed that in my life. It got me through some tough times.

However, softball was my game. I played left field but could fit in where needed. I liked the outfield because I could judge where the ball would go. I could also throw the ball back to almost any base deep in the field. What I loved most was that Mom didn't care that I played it. She hardly came to my games. Mom missed out on glory here because I was all-conference for my junior and senior years. I hit many home runs, got RBIs, stole bases, and played my heart out, and she missed all of it. I still chuckle to this day because she had no idea what the awards I received at our awards banquet were, nor did she ever ask.

I wanted so badly for her to acknowledge me. She could not see past the things she wanted. It was a yearly fight to get her to let me play this sport. She always commented that it would never take me anywhere and I wouldn't play it after high school. What was the sense of putting effort into something like that? All I could think was, then, why was I playing basketball? I was good at it, too, but women's college basketball was only played in some places at a college level during this period. Neither sport was. I was also barrel racing during this time. If I got home late because of softball, she wouldn't let me hear the end of it. I would always train the horses in the evening, especially in the fall, because it was cooler. I don't know if I could have done it any differently. All I know is that I wasn't doing things the right way, her way.

I was doing mediocre in school at this point. I only cared about a few subjects in my freshmen year, and my grades plummeted. Often, I couldn't focus on the class. It all was so boring. I also had so much inner turmoil that it was hard to focus past that. If the class did not interest me, I had a hard time getting the voices of my past to be quiet. I didn't have many "girl" friends at this point; I was socially awkward and had my own opinions, and I guess other girls did not like that. I did have one or two girlfriends, and we understood each other. Mostly, I just gravitated toward guys. They were easy to talk to and would value what I said. They weren't dramatic like the girls. However, I became good friends with one of my girlfriend's boyfriends, Luke. We were naturally pulled toward each other.

We could talk about anything. Luke was a breath of fresh air to me. He would listen to what I was saying and give me feedback. I had never had that, and it made me feel wanted and intelligent. My girlfriend did not like me hanging around him, and in all honesty, my motives were pure. I was not trying to take him from her. I even respected her boundaries and would sit beside her, not him. But he would just talk over her and have a conversation with me. I wanted his friendship, and that was all I wanted from him then. Don't get me wrong. I wanted a boyfriend, but I wanted someone who wanted to get to know me. I wasn't made to be arm candy or play cat and mouse with the boys I went to school with. I was also against my code to steal someone else's boyfriend, and Luke was taken. I had interest and was in relationships, but most of them did not want to know me as a person. Eventually, I would break it off, or they would. My heart longed for someone I could confide in with all the terrible things that

I had gone through. My heart was fragile, and I wasn't about to let just anyone hold it.

I kept being a friend to Luke and wished I would someday have someone like him that I could love. I went through freshman year and that awkward situation between Luke, my friend, and me. I was tired of the games the boys played. I even went after Luke's older brother, who wasn't like Luke and ended up just like the others. I forgot about boys at this and focused on things that would get me out of this place sooner. I got through that year and decided to focus on my studies and get away from here to find people who would want to know me and hear me. That is what I put my eyes on as I went into that summer.

Sam had a sister, Mary, who owned a laundromat/convenience store, and she offered to let me work with her through summer break. She was a kind soul who pushed me to learn how to work. I learned a lot about myself and working for someone else. She helped me to see that everyone treated people differently, and not all of it was bad. She taught me the finer points of having a good work ethic. Most of all, I loved that I could work for money, giving me a sense of freedom. She spoiled me and let me do what I wanted within reason. She let me cook and buy whatever food I wanted. She even took me out to eat a couple of nights a week. This is where I learned that I loved seafood. She was a breath of fresh air for me and treated me like her daughter. She didn't have the pleasure of having kids, and I felt like a daughter to her.

For the summer, she made me forget where I would return to when this time was over. She took me clothes shopping for school. I got to pick out things I wouldn't have had Mom taken me shopping, even if I was spending my money. I remember looking at her and saying there was no way I could pay for these things she told me to pick out. She smiled, said she would handle it, and wanted me to have nice things. I almost started crying right there in the store. Very few people in my life treated me as well as she did. This was the first time that I had bought brand-new clothes since Grandma and Pap took us for that one year. Most of the time, my clothing came from clearance racks at thrift stores. That's not a bad thing, but I rarely got to wear brand-new clothes. A large part of me wished that I really was Mary's daughter and that I could stay here. She had lavished her love on me, and I felt unworthy. She bought me a year's worth of clothing, regular and basketball shoes. Never in my life have I had things that were this nice. She even bought me a suitcase to carry it all back in. She made me feel so loved, not because she bought all those nice things for me, but because she showed me love and care. She made me feel valued.

Sadly, I had to return home a few days after that shopping trip. Mary drove me back, and as soon as I stepped out of the car with all the nice things on, I instantly became the subject of ridicule. I noticed the look of jealousy and anger on my mom's face. I went from a head of high confidence to a little girl who wanted to hide in the corner. She followed me into the house and jumped on me like a cat would a mouse. It went from how dare I spend the money I earned on clothes this expensive to why would I make her pay for all of this? I tried to explain everything, but she wouldn't hear it. Truth be told, I still had every dime I earned. Mary wouldn't let me pay for anything. I bought home a large sum of money that summer, but I wasn't telling my mom that either. It was all cash, and I had to hide it in several places because if Mom found out how much I had, she would find a way to make it hers. When I went out to get the rest of my stuff out of Mary's car, Mom and Sam told Mary that I didn't need any of that and that she wasn't allowed to spend money on me like that. She stretched every bit of her petite frame and stood her ground. Mary said it was her money and she would spend it however she wanted.

She then said something that I had never heard someone say out loud in front of me.

"Amanda is a beautiful girl! She works hard and is nice and kind. You both are so blind to what type of person she is that you are missing out on something great. If you don't open both of your eyes, you will miss out on a relationship with her. I bought her those things because she deserved them. She did everything I asked of her without question, even when she didn't know what I wanted. She makes me wish I had her as my daughter. You will not tell me how I can spend my own money." Mary said with great confidence.

All I could do was stand there in amazement with tears running down my face. Never had someone spoken like that about me. I wished their eyes would have been opened in that split second, but that didn't come. I was told to get into the house and would be talked to later. Why did everything good that happened have to make me feel so bad. I sat upstairs, listening to the conversation continue. Eventually, they calmed down. They agreed I could return next year, but Mary couldn't buy me anything. I was grateful for the agreement and the escape it would give me for next summer. I went about stashing my money everywhere and trying to hide some of the clothes I had, hoping they wouldn't get taken from me.

Thankfully, they never took the clothes from me, but I was always scowled at for what I had on. I felt shame for it and didn't understand what the problem was. What I wore was similar to the clothes Mom had bought Tim. I didn't know why I was being treated this way. There was always a snide remark about how I thought I was better than them now. The truth was, I could no longer wear my other clothes. They were too small, and Mary ensured I had enough to get me through the year. You would think Mom and Sam would have been grateful that they didn't have to pay for anything, but they weren't. I got to where I hated to be around them. I felt such shame because of this. I was so grateful that school started the following week after coming home. It would give me a reason to leave the house and be away from them. So, with the narrow determination to get through school and escape from this place, I went into sophomore year. I stepped into this year not caring about who I was friends with. Luke had a girlfriend, and I wasn't asking for trouble. I stayed away from him and any other boy. I kept to myself. I focused on doing the best I could at school and sports.

I knew I was better than all the lies fed to me. I wanted so much more than what I had been handed in life. My avoidance of Luke put a strain on our friendship. I just couldn't risk the feelings that came when I was with him anymore. I was worried that my feelings for him would grow and that having him would be unattainable. I was also tired of boys playing with my heart and not following through. I wasn't that type of girl. So, I wrote all boys off for the moment and focused on what I wanted to do with my life after I graduated and left this God-forsaken place. I also hadn't heard from God in a while and felt like He had left me. Most of the people that cared for me the most had left. Why wouldn't he, too? I didn't need the distractions anymore; the hurt couldn't hurt anymore because that would overtake me. I told myself I didn't need anyone and that it would be okay to rely on myself.

Looking back, I realize how feeble and foolish those thoughts were. I had grown used to letting people go, but Luke wasn't so willing. He steadily pursued our friendship, even though I avoided him like the plague. I soon realized avoiding him in such a small school would take a lot of work. It was easier to let my guard down a little so I could be friends with him. Conversations resumed as expected, and I was thankful. As much as I hated to admit, Luke was the steadiness I needed. He would make me smile when I was down and always stretch me intellectually. I tried hard to keep it in the friend zone but was falling for him. I looked forward to attending school because I knew he would be there. I couldn't let my feelings show because he was still dating my friend the last I knew.

We spent a lot of time together, and others started noticing. So much so that I was asked constantly throughout the school day. The answer was always the same, he was still in a relationship, and we were just friends. I would receive snide comments, like "It sure looks like you're together." As much as I wanted that to be true, I wasn't trying to steal him. One day, I got asked that question, and I went off. I was so tired of being reminded that I couldn't have him.

The girl I lashed out at looked at me wide-eyed and said, "You don't know, do you?"

"Know what?" I asked, frustrated.

"They haven't been together since the start of school!" she replied.

All I could do was stare at her, apologize for my outburst, and then full realization hit. Luke was available? He never gave me an inkling that he was. Come to think of it, I had not seen him and my friend together in a while. I was so in my head that I had not noticed anything.

The problem was I didn't know one thing about making a move. I was clumsy and awkward any time I tried with other boys. I didn't know how to flirt or even let my intentions known. Things continued as they were. Still in the friend zone, and I didn't know how to make them move further. The questions were still asked, and all I could say was no. I wanted him to make the move so badly because that was how it happened then. Did he not feel what I felt every time I was near him? A classmate got tired of seeing me struggle and tried to set us up. We were in English class, and she came from the back row where Luke sat and asked if I wanted to date him. All I could do was shake my head, yes. She looked at me and said she'd handle it then. She went back there and asked him point blank if he wanted to date me. I watched the transaction, and he shook his head no. She looked at him puzzled, said okay, and then came back to me.

"I suppose you saw his answer?" she asked.

I nodded. Yep, I did. But before I turned around, I looked Luke directly in his eyes to let him see my rejection. Then I saw confusion and the realization of what he had done. I wanted to cry right there in class. Thankfully, the bell rang. I left the class quickly, with tears falling down my face. I heard him calling my name behind me, but I didn't stop. I wanted to put as much distance between him and me as possible. Man, it hurt so much to be rejected that way. By someone I grew close to and wanted to be around.

The girl who orchestrated the conversation tried to console me. I didn't know how to look past this hurt. This hurt was different. I thought he had the same feelings toward me. Had I read more into everything than what was there? This would put a wedge in the friendship, and I constantly asked, did I misjudge everything? The longing looks and always wanting to be next to me in class. I guess I had. It took a couple of months before I felt comfortable enough to be a friend again. I still had feelings for him. In my head, I knew he didn't want me for anything else. Convincing my heart that friendship was all I would get was difficult. I still wanted his friendship, so that's where I would stay. I didn't sit as close, and I was only sometimes as engaging as I was before. I could read from his body language that he was sorry, but I couldn't let myself feel anything for him anymore. I was so tired of feeling hurt on so many levels that the possible hope of a relationship with him had to die. I had to move on and become focused on my original plan.

About this time, another boy started to show interest in me. He would flirt with me in class but not in front of his friends. I know it was wrong, but I enjoyed those times with him. I wanted something else, but it would do for right now. I didn't want to feel the hurt, and these times distracted me from that. I didn't want a relationship with him, but it felt good to feel wanted. I knew he was toying with me. I wasn't blind, but when I had his attention, it let me forget about Luke. This was the cycle that I went through for a few months. It escalated slightly, but not enough for him to move past the flirting and attention.

Valentine's Day was approaching, and I secretly hoped for something from him. The boys' basketball team sold carnations that year for a fundraiser. I was told that my name was on a flower. I got excited because I thought the boy would make his move. I was in science class when my flower walked through the door.

I looked at the boy and mouthed, "Did you do this?"

He shrugged. I read the note, and my heart sank. Will you go out with me? Signed Luke. So many emotions ripped through my body. I looked at Luke and then the other boy. I had worked so hard to repair my friendship with Luke. Honestly, I didn't want anything to damage it. I was tired of being in the friend zone with both. I wanted more, and mainly with Luke. The problem was I didn't want to lose our friendship. I needed him as a friend. Despite what I was going through, he cared, and I didn't want to lose that. I wrote him a note saying I just wanted to be friends. I knew it would crush him, but I couldn't lose him as a friend if the relationship didn't work out.

For the next two weeks, I agonized over that decision. Our friendship had changed, and it was my fault this time. We didn't seek each other out anymore and only talked if we were near one another. It hurt me to watch the friendship start to fall apart. One of our friends noticed the situation between us. She asked what was going on. I told her everything down to being shown affection by another boy, hoping he would make a move. As I stood there choking back tears, she asked what I wanted from this. Realization hit me, it was Luke. I had always wanted Luke. I wanted his love, warmth, and touch; I wanted everything. He is the only one in my life who made me feel that there was more than all the pain that I had gone through. She then asked why I didn't go after that. All I could do was shrug. She then said that I could change that. So that's what I did when I went home that night. I hadn't prayed in a long time, but I hoped God was listening. I asked for guidance on what to write and prayed again, hoping it was right and he would agree and be mine.

I was so scared the next day. I tried to talk myself into handing it to him, but I chickened out. So, during lunch, I snuck up to the class where he had left his bag. In the process, one of the guys in our class saw me. He asked what I was doing, and I told him I was trying to find Luke's bag. He walked over to it and opened it. I slipped the note and my class ring into his shoe. I said another prayer that he would agree. The guy then said something that dumbfounded me.

"I hope that was a note saying you'll be his girlfriend." he motioned toward the bag.

I nodded.

"Good. Watching you two try to get together has been agonizing. I almost thought it wasn't going to happen." The guy confessed

I looked at him and whispered, "Hopefully, it does."

Unfortunately, that was on a Friday, and I would have to wait until Monday to find his answer. But that is what I get by not giving it to him personally. He would have an away basketball game, so I wouldn't even see him at practice. It was all I could do to concentrate on school or basketball, let alone wonder how I would make it through the weekend. (We didn't have smartphones at this point in history. If we did, I'm sure Mom would not have let me have one.) I'm an over-thinker, and I ran every possible scenario through my head as to how this would go and slept very little. I was thankful for once for all the chores I had to do. They kept my mind occupied. I prayed that he would say yes and we would be happy together. I wanted that more than I had wanted anything in my life.

Monday came, and with hope in my heart, I walked through the school doors. He wouldn't be there yet; he lived twenty minutes from the school and rode the bus when I was driven or drove every day. I waited anxiously for him to walk through the doors. Hoping against hope that he would want to be with me as much as I wanted him. He finally came through the doors, and the first thing I noticed was a huge smile, and then he had my ring on his neck. He came and sat next to me, and for the first time all year, there was this easiness between us.

"So, I got your note." A smile spread across my face, and even though I knew the answer, hearing it would be much better.

"And?"

He leaned in close, and I could feel his breath on my skin, and it gave me chills, "Yes, the answer is yes."

I couldn't help but smile one of those cheek-hurting smiles. It's all I did for the next few days. Even my Mom and Sam's attitudes toward me couldn't make me stop smiling, and they did try. I even heard them muttering in confusion about why I was acting that way. Luke was the light in the darkness that I needed. He made me feel wanted and valuable. I had rarely been treated that way until we became friends. I finally had someone in my corner, and even though I was afraid to share everything I had endured early on, I knew that someday I could share with him. I felt like I could eventually trust him.

It wasn't long before others noticed we spent more time together and dating. Especially the other boy. He practically became unraveled in one of our classes together.

He looked at me with an insulting face and said through clenched teeth, "Why would you pick him over me? I guess you are both the same, fat and ugly!"

I looked at him dumbfounded. I was neither, and I had abs. My brain moves very fast when I'm angry. What I said next sat him down, and he didn't say anything to me for quite a while.

"I waited weeks for you to make a move on me, but I guess I was only good enough for you when your friends weren't around. If you wanted me so badly, you should have sucked it up and made a move. By the way, we are neither of those things! Have you bothered to look at your body lately?" I yelled.

With that last line, his face turned bright red, and I could almost see the steam coming out of his ears.

"Do you have anything else you would like to say to me? No, I didn't think so, and before you say another word about me to anyone else, you better make sure it's right! I will hunt you down and embarrass you in front of your precious friends that I wasn't good enough for!" I continued.

With each statement, my frustrations with him showed. When I finished, the whole class was quiet, including the teacher. I turned and went to my seat, and in the process, everyone started clapping.

One of the girls I always sat next to looked at me and laughingly said, "You're amazing! I didn't know you had it in you."

I grinned, "There's a lot about me you don't know."

She shrugged, "Probably so, but he deserved that. I hated how he treated you, and you let him do it."

She was right, but I was lonely and liked the attention. Yes, it was wrong, but my mindset was different then. While dating Luke, that mindset shifted to things that would be great for me if I allowed them to happen. Luke moved slowly, and I was okay with that. It's like he knew I needed that. It was so comforting to be in his embrace; I felt protected and thoroughly enjoyed his warmth. We held hands, and he would walk with his arm around me. It took him three months just to kiss me. I did give him ample opportunities, but it needed to be right for him. I had kissed other boys, but his kiss set me on fire. I started to have feelings for him that I had never experienced before, and I didn't know what to do with them. Love wasn't familiar to me, but I knew I was falling for him. Do you know those beginning stages of love that make you feel like someone took your insides, shook them harshly, and then gave them back? Yeah, that was me, and honestly, it scared me. I didn't know what to do with all those feelings. I had been in survival mode most of my life, and it wouldn't allow me to act that way. Luke was bringing me out of that. I couldn't focus unless it was on him. Usually, I could clear all the chatter in my head and focus on the task or sport at hand. However, when I did that, Luke would come busting through and completely wreck any thought I had. I wanted to be near him every minute of the day at school.

Weekends were terrible because I wasn't allowed to see him much. I couldn't call him either because Sam would pick up the phone and listen. Mom would have to know ahead of time. Then, I would have to compete with chores or her schedule to be able to go. Mind you, I had my driver's license and a truck. Finally, I would get the good girl routine. You know, if you're a good girl, then you can go. When we reached the end of the school year, I knew it would be a while before I could see him. I was going back to Mary's for the summer. I didn't want to leave him, but the money I would earn would help me get through the year. I also knew she would take care of me. We exchanged addresses, promising to write. We wrote to each other every week.

It was the same with Mary as the previous year, but she gave me more independence. I would run errands for her to ease her workload, and she loved me for it. Just like the year before, she bought my clothes. I tried to stop her, but she wouldn't hear it. How was I going to keep these clothes this year? I had to fight Mom last year to keep what Mary had already given me. Like the year before, I got ridiculed, and Mary stood up for me. When I was with her this time, I noticed Mary wasn't as plucky as she had always been. She seemed to tire out quickly. Granted, she was in her sixties, but last year, she gave me a run for my money on energy. I was physically fit and struggled to keep up with her. This year, she

My gut told me this would be the last time I could work with her. I learned soon after summer was over she had cancer. I wanted to go and see her, but Mom and Sam wouldn't take me or even go see her by themselves. She had to sell everything she owned because she no longer could take care of everything. She gave Sam all her yard equipment, which was more than he deserved. I overheard Mom and Sam both complaining that they weren't getting any money from her. Mary was moving to Florida near one of their sisters since Sam wouldn't help take care of her. That was the last I saw of Mary. It hurt deeply that I couldn't tell her how much she meant to me or how valuable her knowledge was. I wanted to thank her for all the things she did for me. I didn't deserve the kindness she showed. I don't know if she realized how grateful I was for it.

My junior year continued like the end of my Sophomore year. Luke and I grew in our relationship and learned how to work the system with my mom, which was ever-changing. I was in the homecoming court, and we went to prom. We both excelled at school and sports. There wasn't anything that we couldn't face together. He introduced me to his family and people at his church. And even though I was apprehensive about meeting new people, they made me feel like family.

Senior year, however, was a different story. Mom had become more and more agitated with Luke being my boyfriend. She started to hate the thought of me dating him and would take any moment to let me know her annoyance. To be honest, Mom and Sam were not getting along either. He always complained about money and the number of animals she brought home. I had gained an enormous chore list but didn't complain because I could go out with Luke if I completed them. Also, I had turned 18 not too far into the school year, and Mom was losing my social security income from Tony. I didn't ever see a dime from it, but either way, she was losing it and wasn't happy about it. Mom also started blaming me for her and Sam's relationship. She would say that Sam didn't like Luke. Or that my attitude was the reason that we would be kicked out. While it was true, Sam didn't like Luke. I didn't show that much attitude towards Sam. I did stand my ground, but I was not disrespectful to him. I did my best, but how are you supposed to handle someone who says everything I did was wrong? Including but not limited to horses, sports, the way I dressed (I dressed modestly), and so on. He had no experience in those areas, so I often told him what I thought. For instance, I had a barrel racing horse that did not need encouragement to run. If you wore spurs, she would get nervous and was extremely hard to handle. One night, barrel racing, Mom kept telling me that Sam said I needed to wear the spurs to make her go faster. I didn't ride horses that needed extra equipment to make them do something. I worked hard with this mare, and she was in top condition. I had to prove a point as much as I didn't want to.

I apologized to my mare, and I climbed into the saddle. That horse showed out in grand fashion. She reared up, bucked, and was everywhere in that arena but where she needed to be. Halfway through the barrel pattern, I gave up. She had already knocked over two barrels and almost the third. I had already been in the arena for thirty seconds, double my usual time. I went toward the stands, took the spurs off, and threw them at Mom and Sam. I then went to the announcer stand and asked for a reset. I was not leaving that arena until I showed them what this horse could do. My mare had calmed down and was acting completely normal. I leaned forward in the saddle and petted her neck, encouraging her. A reset meant no points or time would be recorded, but it was allowed when a horse messed up this bad. She performed beautifully; she did the pattern perfectly. It was her best time, but it wouldn't count. I know I made both of them mad, but the truth must be shown.

I knew what that horse could do, and she did it willingly. Nothing extra is needed. As I finished the run, tears were streaming down my face. I faulted this mare. She would have won that night. I couldn't let Sam keep telling me what to do when I knew the horse better than anyone else. Mom was waiting at the trailer, and I could tell her face was red before I arrived. I got off the horse, and as I was tying her to the trailer, she smacked me upside the head so hard it bounced off the trailer. I hated being hit that way; it instantly made me angry. Of course, I was in trouble for what I did. No one would listen to me, and I had the horse to think of. I had to bite my tongue while I listened to her rant. With tears and a throbbing head, I said nothing and took care of my horse. People stopped to watch the scene. I noticed that she had raised her hand again to hit me again. I turned around and caught it. Through clenched teeth, I told her to stop. She started to raise her other hand, and I squeezed the one in my other hand until she yelped.

"Do not hit me again! I am only concerned about the horse I treated badly because of you!" I practically spit through clenched teeth.

"She would have won if you hadn't insisted on me wearing those stupid spurs! No one listens to me even though I always ride her." I continued.

She still had her hand raised. A passerby stopped and asked if I needed help.

Mom started to whine for help, but I stared her down and said, "No sir, everything is fine!"

I hadn't had a confrontation with Mom like this in a long time. I knew it was coming; I didn't know it would be tonight. She had increasingly gotten more and more hateful with me and kept pushing the envelope to see what she could get away with. Being inexperienced with these things, I let her keep going until she made me erupt.

I finally let her go, and she stomped off, rubbing her hand. I knew for sure she was going to tattle on me to Sam. I didn't care then, nor would anything come from her telling him. I sank to the ground against the trailer and tried to settle the anger that had risen up in me. I had someone to listen to me, but not having him here made me feel lonely. How many more days until I was free from her? I was a senior in high school, so there weren't many. Then my mare nudged my shoulder with her nose, reminding me she still needed to be taken care of. I felt so bad for doing that to her. She didn't deserve to be treated that way. I just needed them to see. I got up and gave her a hug. She started head-butting me to get the bridle off. She seemed to have already forgotten the incident. I started removing her tack and then brushed her down. She kept reaching for grass, so I fed her hay and sweet grain from the trailer. I so badly needed someone to talk to at that moment.

I sat back down and just prayed to God. He had always been there, and I poured my heart out to him. My mare had finished eating, and I loaded her into the trailer. The rodeo would be over soon, and I didn't want to give them a reason to speak to me. I doubted they would let me ride in the truck's cab, so I got a blanket out of the front, climbed into the bed, and fell asleep. It wasn't until morning that I realized they had just left me out there after we got home. I wasn't mad because it was one of the most peaceful nights of sleep I had in a while. I made my way slowly out of the bed of the truck. I was groggy and needed a change of clothes and to go to the bathroom. I was on the front porch and heard yelling inside the house. I didn't want to go in, but my bladder screamed for attention. I knew if I walked in, all attention would turn to me, and then, most likely, some sort of blame. I couldn't stand there any longer. I had to go. So I slowly turned the knob and slipped in the door. They weren't in the part of the house where the bathroom was, so I went quickly. I was able to sneak back out the door, or so I thought.

"Amanda!" Mom yelled.

I turned to face her, "Yes?"

"You need to get your horse out of the trailer," she said devilishly.

I turned and looked at the trailer, and there she still was. The poor thing, I didn't even hear her when I got out of the truck. I started for the trailer with Mom rattling off everything I would have to do that day, nothing unusual. It was Saturday, and she had me doing everything she could think of.

"Oh, and one more thing, with that stunt you pulled last night, you will not see Luke tonight." She spoke.

I could almost hear her twisted smile; I was right when I turned around.

"That's okay. Luke has to work this weekend." I said, happier than I felt.

She looked momentarily deflated but ended with, "At least he's good for something."

She knew she would hit her mark with that statement, but I couldn't let her see the pain it caused.

"Is there anything else, or can I get started?" I asked.

She shook her head and smiled as she went back inside.

At this point, it wasn't worth getting changed, but I needed a T-shirt instead of a Western shirt. I made my way upstairs from the outside. I wanted so badly to sink into my pillow and cry, but I wouldn't give her the satisfaction of hearing me sobbing. I grabbed an old shirt from my closet and changed. I also needed a bath, but that wouldn't happen until this evening. I searched my gym bag for a granola bar and grabbed the water jug I kept upstairs. It wasn't much, but it will work for right now, and hopefully, I can get a meal sometime today. I would likely have to make it myself because Mom didn't cook much on Saturday. I went back outside and down the stairs.

First, to the trailer and to let my horse out. Since last night, she had had nothing to eat besides her hay bag and feed. I wondered why they would be so cruel to her, but I knew the answer. It was me. I was the reason that they left her in the trailer. I unlatched the trailer door, and she came willingly to the door. She was ready to break free. I got her out, and she started dancing around me, impatiently waiting for me to take her halter off. She started neighing, trying to locate the rest of the herd. It took me a minute, but I finally got her loose from the halter. She took off at a dead run towards the pond when she realized she was free of the halter. She drank her fill and began trying to locate the others.

I could hear their footfalls coming from the back of the property. They greeted the mare with the familiarity of sniffs, jumps, and neighs. The herd greatly accepted her and showed how much they missed her. It was an awe-inspiring scene, but it made me tear up. I longed for a family like that. I know that they were horses, but she had something I didn't. I had Luke, but it would be months before we could be more independent, and I needed to escape from my mom. I was on the other side of the trailer and knew no one else was out there. I let the tears unashamedly fall. The pain had to go somewhere, and I was having trouble holding it all in. I sat on the edge of the trailer and let the body quaking sobs come and the white-hot tears fall.

I just wanted to be loved and accepted for who I was. I was supposed to be a "good girl" and "work hard." I couldn't even have a job because I was too valuable on the farm. I had a small stash from working with Mary, but Mom had helped herself to what she could find. I just wanted Mom to love me, but to her, I was a slave. I was so ready to be free from her. I was angry that she made my horse stay in the trailer all night. She was supposed to love these animals, but she didn't take of them; I did. I wondered if she would have all these animals if she didn't have me caring for them. I added one more item to the list because she had left my horse in the trailer overnight. The horse trailer needed cleaning because my mare had made a mess of it. So, I stood up and got to work. While it helped to cry, it didn't solve anything, nor did the chores magically disappear. I moved the truck further into the field and scooped the piles of poop out into the field.

We didn't use the poop for fertilizer, so it was often tossed in the field. I then moved the trailer over by a hose, sprayed it out, put it back where it went and unloaded the tack. When that was done, I cleaned cages and fed and watered our animals. Sam would sit on the porch swing and watch me work, most likely reporting to Mom. He wouldn't say anything to me but would sit there and swing the entire time, watching the comings and goings of his land. He liked watching all the animals, but he was right. We had too many. To say that to Mom, though, was an abomination.

I never understood why there were always so many animals. Mom didn't pay much attention to them other than the dogs she was allowed to keep in the house. I rarely saw her outside taking care of them. Why did she need so many? Was it a possession thing? The more you have, the better? That's an answer that I would never know. With everything that I needed to get done on Saturdays, it took well into the afternoon, and I was often exhausted, and today was no exception. I needed food and a bath, but a bath would have to come first. I smelled like every one of the animals that I cleaned up after that day. Sam complained of my smell when I walked past him.

"I know I can't stand the smell of myself; I'm fixing to take care of it," I said.

He smiled a little bit, and I went inside. I was greeted with the smell of cooking. Was Mom cooking on Saturday? My stomach couldn't help itself but growl; I was hungry. I turned to the bathroom to start a bath and then went to get a clean change of clothes. I was hopeful that there was some food for me, but knowing my mom's attitude right now, there probably wasn't. She stopped me on my way back.

"You smell awful!" she said as she waved her hand in front of her face.

I thought that if she went out and cared for those animals herself, she would understand the conditions I had to clean every week.

I looked at her and said, "I'm going to take care of that right now. The water is running in the bathtub."

The same grin came across her face from this morning, "Oh, and you will need to cook dinner for yourself. I only made enough for me and Sam."

I shrugged and said, "Okay."

That was not enough of a reaction for her, so she told me what her dinner was, and again I said, "Okay."

While she was trying to come up with something else to say, I pushed past her, went into the bathroom, set my things down, turned off the water, and came back out. I didn't care at that moment if I stunk. I needed to lay out meat. I went to the freezer, grabbed a couple of chicken breasts, and put them in the sink to thaw; all the while, Mom complained of my smell. She brought it on herself because I needed to eat, and the meat needed to be thawed.

"I will go and take a bath now," I announced.

That must have brought great relief to her, but she was busy waving the smell out of the room. As I sank into the bathwater, I had a smirk on my face. She didn't realize I liked to cook, and I loved cooking for myself. I didn't know how to cook much from scratch because all mom would buy was prepackaged food. But there was stuff like flour, butter, eggs, and some seasonings.

As I thought about what to cook, I sank further into the bathwater. I let the warmth of the water seep into my muscles. This was the best I had felt all day. I was physically tired, and the bath felt terrific. I washed from my head to my toes and got out. I always disliked it when the bath was over. It often felt like a respite for me. No one bothered me while I was there, and I could let my mind wander to better things. I dressed in clean clothes, took the dirty ones to the laundry room, and checked on the chicken I laid out. It wasn't quite thawed, so I gathered more laundry to do.

The meat thawed, and I decided to make fried chicken with it. I didn't know how to fry chicken, but Mom did it, so how hard could it be. I made an egg wash and a flour mixture with the spices I found around the kitchen. I dipped the chicken in the egg, then the flour, and left it there while the oil heated. I wanted mashed potatoes, but not the boxed kind. Anna, Luke's Mom, made mashed potatoes from scratch, and that was what I wanted. I found 2 large potatoes, peeled and chopped them. Then, I dropped the chopped potatoes into a pot with water and let them boil. Vegetables were more challenging to find, but we had canned goods. I was able to find canned corn and cooked it, too. When the oil was hot, I dropped the chicken in. Everything smelled amazing. So much so that both Sam and Mom came to the kitchen to inspect. Mom turned her nose up at it, but I could tell Sam's dinner had left him wanting.

He looked at me and asked, almost pleading, "Would it be possible for you to share a little of what you're making?"

I had planned on saving some for tomorrow because cooking wasn't done on Sunday either, but I felt sorry for him.

"I won't need much, but it smells good." He commented.

I looked at him and said, "Yep, I'll share some."

I always cooked on Saturdays for myself, but he would often ask if I could make extra. That was a meager fare compared to this. It was usually boxed noodles, premade hamburger patties, or mashed potatoes from a box. Everything tasted wonderful, and I could tell by

Sam's face and the plate I made for him that he was enjoying it, too. Mom did not touch it, though; I could see her looking with longing toward us at the table. I cleaned up afterward and hid what I had left in the fridge. At that moment, I felt confident in my ability to cook. I went after that, finished my laundry, and took it upstairs. All the while, Mom glared at me like I did something wrong. When I got upstairs, I sat on my bed to fold clothes. I was tired but felt good about what I accomplished with dinner. Mom's glare couldn't take away my confidence right then.

For the first time I could remember, I looked upward and said, "Thank you for making me feel better!"

I felt God smiling at me in return.

We left Sam's after Christmas that year. I was told that we were being kicked out. Mom sold off a lot of animals and their things. I never knew if she wanted to leave or if Sam was kicking us out. I just know I got blamed for the reason. Which was not true. Honestly, Sam and I were getting along. It was all the animals that were everywhere. That was often what they fought about; I rarely heard my name brought up during those times. I just know we had a place to live one day, and the next, we were out on our own.

The truck Mom had got re-possessed. She talked me into trading in the truck Grandma and Pap bought me to get a larger truck. My grandparents were distraught at her for that. I had no choice but to go along. Mom's credit was terrible, but the car dealership took mine. It was all in the name of helping Mom and hoping to gain her favor. I felt I was giving my independence away when I signed those papers. I felt bad for Mom and the predicament we were in. She barely made that payment as well because a banker from the local bank showed up at school. Getting pulled out of class was embarrassing because your name was on the loan, but you could not pay for it. I was truly stuck. She wouldn't let me get a job, but she did not care that she was destroying my credit. I told the banker what had happened, and he raised his eyebrows. He said he would try to extend the furlough period for a couple of months but couldn't promise any more time. Many people saw me talking to him, and I was asked many questions. I really couldn't bring myself to say anything to anyone but Luke. I was dumbfounded, and I didn't know what to do.

The first place we moved to had a small pasture, but it wasn't big enough to feed our horses for long. The landlord didn't want the horses there anyway because they were ruining the small field, which was true. But Mom fed him a sob story that she didn't have anywhere for them to go. They gave us a time limit of two weeks, but Mom ran it over by a month or two. I had become sick in the months that we were there. I'm not sure how it started other than I got very wet while feeding the horses one evening while Mom was out running around. I woke up the following day with this unbearable pain in my throat and neck, and I could barely swallow. My breath stunk like I had something dead in my mouth. Mom yelled at me to get up, and I didn't budge. She kept yelling and then finally came into my room.

"Why does it smell so bad in here?" she said.

"Mom, I'm sick." I choked out.

"Oh, you'll feel better. Just get out of bed." Mom commanded.

I did as I was told, thinking that I could make it. I sat up and hung my feet over the bed. My head throbbed horribly. I willed the headache to go away and tried to stand up. I wasn't two steps from the bed, and everything went black. I must have passed out because the next thing I remember was Mom standing over me, yelling like she was scared. Looking at her, I saw real worry in her eyes for me.

"Can you get up?" she asked.

I just looked at her, not comprehending what she was saying. My head was throbbing so badly. I just wanted to go back to sleep. I wanted my bed. I crawled back to it and pulled myself in while Mom said something I still wasn't hearing. Once I got under the blankets, I fell asleep again, never hearing what she said. I woke up sometime later, and my throat was on fire. I was very thirsty. I was afraid to get out of bed, so I called for Mom. Nothing. Maybe she was just outside taking care of the animals. I waited a little bit longer and called again, but nothing. The thirst was insistent.

I was going to have to get out of bed to get some water. I moved slower, this time clutching the wall where I could. I shuffled to the kitchen to get a glass of water. The fire grew hotter in my throat with each swallow, but I was so thirsty. I needed to use the bathroom as well. I was slowly on my way to the bathroom when I glanced outside. I didn't see the truck there. I instantly grew angry, and tears sprung into my eyes. Did I even matter to her? Obviously not! My head couldn't make sense of it. I got done in the bathroom and headed back to my room. Every ounce of energy I had was taken by that, and I fell back in bed to sleep. I woke up to the sound of the door opening.

"Mom?" I asked.

"No, it's me." came a man's voice, and I welcomed it.

It was Luke. He had come to check on me and wondered why I wasn't in school. He was on his way to work but spared a few minutes to check on me.

"What's the matter?" he asked.

"My throat is on fire, and I can't move without my head throbbing," I responded weakly.

Just him caring about me made me feel better.

"I don't have long, but can I get you anything?" He asked.

"Could you help me to the bathroom and get me some more water?" I said weakly.

He willingly reached for me and helped me out of bed. When I stood up, he hugged me, and I sank into his warmth. He kissed me on the forehead and helped me to the bathroom. While in the bathroom,

I could hear him rummaging around in the kitchen. He returned and knocked on the door to see if I needed help. I opened the door and smiled weakly at him. He helped me back to my room and asked if I knew if there was any chicken noodle soup or something soft he could heat up in the microwave for me to eat. I shook my head. The last thing on Mom's mind was ensuring we had food. Money was tight, and she had animals to feed.

He got me to the edge of my bed and sat with me, "I need to be going. Is there anything else you need before I leave?"

"No," I said weakly.

I wished I could tell him how grateful I was for him just stopping by to show he cared. As he stood up to go, I heard the front door open. Worry came to my mind. He kissed me again on the forehead, turned, and met my mom at the door. Even at 18, Luke was twice the size of my mom. She just moved and let him pass. She stood there watching him until the door closed and glared at me.

Through clenched teeth, she said, "What was he doing here?"

I started lying down and said, "He was just checking on me and making sure I was okay."

I turned over and was asleep before I could hear her response. The following two days were spent the same way, with Luke checking on me, and I wasn't getting any better. On the third day, I pleaded with Mom to take me to the doctor. I had not eaten in 3 days, nor could I. I felt like my throat was swelling to the point I could barely swallow. I just wanted to feel better. She eventually took me to the doctor. He said I had strep throat, and it was the worst case he had seen in a while. My mom went into the room with me. I really couldn't say anything about how she took care of me. She would deny everything and say I was out of my mind because I was sick. The doctor said that if I had gone much longer, I would have been hospitalized to get the infection under control. He also said that I wasn't allowed to go back to school until the puss pockets in my throat were gone. By the look on her face, Mom was angry, but she nodded.

"Amanda has to take the antibiotics, or she will be hospitalized. I am also giving her something for the pain so that she can eat. I will send the prescriptions over to our pharmacy. Please make sure that she gets them."

As he said this, he looked at me the whole time. As if he knew what I went through. I slightly nodded and looked away. I couldn't tolerate the way he stared at me. I felt great shame. I was too scared to talk to anyone about the hell I had gone through with her. I didn't have anyone other than Luke; he knew bits and pieces but not everything. I was scared to show him all the scars I had. We were forced to stay in the waiting room until one of the nurses brought me the antibiotics and cough syrup. She sat beside me, showing me what the bottles said and how to take them. I understood everything and nodded as we went. She then leaned forward and acknowledged Mom.

"Mom, she needs food to regain her strength, like chicken soup, scrambled eggs, soft foods, and Gatorade. Amanda is dehydrated and needs the extra care you can give her. You must get her some food before you go home so her stomach doesn't get upset when she takes this. She will need to stay home from school until the pustules and fever are gone, okay?" The nurse asked.

My mom didn't like her assignment but agreed and asked when I needed to take everything. The nurse repeated everything, giving emphasis to making sure I had food. We left the doctor's office. I had my medicine in hand; I wasn't sure I would get them if they were given to Mom. She said nothing, but I read Mom's body language and knew she was frustrated. We got in the truck, and she sat for a moment. I saw her shoulders drop in resignation. She looked at me and asked what I wanted to eat.

"I would like some soup and mashed potatoes, please," I said barely above a whisper.

"I will stop and get food for the house and then head home. I have animals to take care of," she said insistently.

And that's what she did. For the next week, she took care of me. I tried not to read anything into it, but I did appreciate it. I was afraid to get used to it, but it felt normal in our house between the two of us. She made sure I was eating and drinking the Gatorade and asked if I was taking the medicine the doctor gave me. She gave me extra blankets for my bed and ensured I stayed warm. Luke stopped by as much as he could to check on me. I was getting better slowly, and the pustules had gone away. Luke asked if I wanted to go out on Saturday, and Mom said I could.

That night, when he picked me up, Mom was not home. Luke stepped through the doorway with a small velvet box in his hand. I instantly started to argue with him, saying we said we would wait. He just shushed me, saying this was just a promise ring.

"This is my promise to you, and I want you as my wife." He said as he slipped the ring on my finger.

I just stared at it in awe. No one had ever done something so nice for me. I started to cry, and Luke gathered me into his arms. I wished I could have, but I didn't know how to tell him how thankful I was for him. He gave me so much hope when I didn't seem to have any. We went and had a great date that night. It was mostly just us talking and laughing and loving one another. When he dropped me off that night and I walked through the door, there was a noticeable shift in the house. Gone were the good feelings from the last week, replaced with something dark and familiar. I knew that this would be back. It always came back like a familiar friend I didn't want. I shook the feeling of despair from my mind. It was not going to pull me down tonight. I had a promise to look forward to, which would carry me through.

We moved two more times before the end of my senior year. The next place was nicer, but no animals were allowed. Our stay there lasted only a short time. I never knew why, but Mom couldn't live without the animals. The next place we moved in the last month of high school was for me. However, it was closer to where Luke lived, so we got to see each other more. Tim was also graduating college and was given assignments for the Air Force and a sign-on bonus. Mom had bought him a car before college and somehow managed to pay for it. He brought it back home and said that I could have it. I was thankful that I had something to drive again. Tim had bought a Jeep, so that was the reason he gave me the car. Mom had thought about selling it but asked if she could keep it so I could get a job. The place we moved to was a ranch, and Mom worked for the owner. She had a place to put her horses now and could get some animals. I had moved away from doing chores all the time and focused on finishing high school.

It was such an exciting and sad time in my life. This was the one place I had stayed this long in my entire life. I had a support network here, and I saw Luke daily. Every year, Seniors would get to go on a trip with the funds and points they had earned over the year. We were going to Pensacola, Florida, and Gulf Shores, Alabama. I was very excited; I hadn't been outside Missouri in a long time. The class rented a charter bus for the trip there. I couldn't wait to spend time with Luke alone without having to work so hard to see him.

We would be free to do what we wanted when we got there. We spent most of our time together having fun or hanging out. I let the worries of my home life just fade into the background. Life would have to wait until I got back home. We were gone for a week, then came back to practice graduation. I got overly emotional when we got back, and I almost broke up with Luke because of it. There were too many unknowns, and I wanted a planned course. I was accepted to a college, but I had yet to learn past that. Luke and I were also thinking about getting married, which worried me. I could not see the best-case scenario or how anything would work out. I had never had freedom of choice before. I didn't know how to sift any of it. In a moment of craziness, I almost let go of the one thing that made me feel human. My sanity came back. I apologized, and he was forgiving. He's always forgiving.

He looked at me and said, "Everything will be okay. We will figure it out."

I wish graduation was a special time, but it wasn't. I was made to feel like I was a failure the entire time. My family came to watch, and I was told I should have won more awards. I didn't make valedictorian or salutatorian, but I was seventh in my class. I felt accomplished, regardless of what my family told me. Would they have done that well if they had walked the same path I did to reach that point? No one knew about my life and the abuse that I had gone through. I desperately hoped that one-day things would change, and I would be asked about my raising instead of assumptions being made.

**Disclaimer:** I want you to understand I was not a perfect child. I did have an attitude; I did talk back and would fight back against what was happening to me most of the time. A lot of it stemmed from the abuse I had gone through. I am strong-willed and stubborn and often would remind them this was wrong. It never ended well and would most likely get me punished because no one likes their faults pointed out. I did dabble in smoking and alcohol, but I hated both. I did things I shouldn't have done; I'm saying this to show you I was not perfect by any standard. I wasn't taught how to handle all the emotions I was dealing with. I was taught to stuff them down and keep going like nothing happened. I was intimate with Luke but didn't talk about that because even though this is a story of my life, it is very personal to me.

I regret our actions because they should have been saved for marriage. I loved him and thought doing those things showed that. I often can't help but wonder what it would have been like had we waited.

## Pivot Point:

As I was writing this chapter, God revealed his love for me. I can look back now and see that God intricately placed people in my life to help me get through these years. Mary treated me like a daughter even though she didn't give birth to me. She gave to me lavishly and abundantly and did this despite what was said. I experienced things with her that I have not done with anyone else to this point in life. Luke came into my life and gave me a friend. Even though I did not feel free to explain what I had been through, he accepted me as a person. He brought out the good parts of myself and made me feel accepted. Luke would be the one that God promised to bring into my life, that would help heal my hurts. Both Luke and Mary came into my life when I was hurting and continuously being hurt.

> *The name of the Lord is a strong fortress: the godly run to him and are safe.* **Proverbs 18:10**

They were the safe havens I needed during this time. God knew what I needed. He put these people in my life to show that He was there. Even though I didn't fully understand who He was. Most of my relationship with Him would be spent holding Him at arms' length because trust would be an issue I would have to overcome. Trusting God did not come easy when he was someone I could not tangibly touch.

# CHAPTER 6

# Adulthood: Overcoming My Childhood

**ADMITTEDLY, THIS WAS** a hard transition for me. Not in the manner that I was too scared to become an adult. I was more than ready to stand on my own two feet. Mom started acting differently than I was accustomed to. It went from wanting total inclusion to abandonment. Yes, I realize that I was 18, but she helped Tim every step of the way. This should not have bothered me at this point, but it did. I still had this unfailing hope that she would favor me someday. With becoming an adult, my guard was still up, but I couldn't judge situations as well as I used to. She would often hurl arrows of hurt toward me to see where they would create the most damage. Being in her household was safer than being away from it. I was very naive and wanted to believe the best about her. I had this ideology of the person that my mom could be. I had seen it so often with Tim, sometimes for me. Why did I fall through the cracks with her? Early in life, I had no choice who was picked to be my father, but she did. I had no choice in the way Tony treated me through my childhood. None of that could be helped by me, and I didn't want any of it. Life was hard with Tony and not any easier with her.

My life with them was a vacuum of madness that I couldn't pull myself from. I wanted out of it but kept going back to the familiar. My mom's love for me would become this roller coaster madness that was good one minute and bad the next. Why didn't I walk away? Because I held on to the hope that she would eventually become this loving mother I had dreamed of. Adulthood has been strange to navigate without strong parental figures to pattern my life after. My life became ideas of who I didn't want to be as a woman and eventually a parent.

Luke and I married close to Christmas, the same year after graduation. Mom voiced her opinion about Luke every chance she got. Her ranting just became something I didn't listen to anymore. She had moved into the main house on the farm she worked for. I suspected she was bedding the man who owned the farm, but I never said anything. She had quit buying food and needed items for the house. I was taking care of myself at this point. I had a job and could buy some food, but not much other than the gas I needed to get to work. I eventually moved in with Luke's mom and dad through a series of unforeseen events. Mom had found another man suddenly and was leaving; I wasn't allowed to stay there anymore. She wanted me gone quickly. I had spent that week after she shared the news moving things. I had a little left to get, and I would be gone. That Sunday was my last day in that place. Mom was furious that I was going to church when I needed to finish packing. I didn't have much left, and God was essential to me now. Luke had started taking me to church every Sunday since I moved closer. She barricaded herself up against the front door, blocking my way. I tried to talk to her like an adult, but there was no reason with her.

"Please move, I need to leave," I said, barely hiding my frustration.

"You think that you are all high and mighty going to church, don't you?" she condescendingly.

"No, I don't, and you could come with me, learn about God, maybe get saved," I said.

"You think I'm going to hell, don't you?" she asked.

In my inexperience, I answered the question the best I knew how and told the truth. I started crying in frustration, which did not help what came next. In my short time attending church, I learned to judge the fruits. She didn't show outward signs like Tony, so I answered honestly.

"I think so. Please come to church with me," I pleaded.

I barely got the whole sentence out before she smacked me upside the head. She always went for my head, and it sparked anger in me. No more would she ever hit me like that. Before I realized it, my hand smacked her upside the head as well. I don't know who was more surprised, me or her. Years of her hitting me like that were over; I was no longer that little girl she could treat like this.

"You will no longer hit me in any way. I will be out of this place by day's end. Now, move out of my way. I have somewhere to be." I said with more power than I felt.

A startled look came across, questioning what her next move should be. I stared her down. If this was going to happen, I was ready. If she wanted a fight, I would give it to her. I was exhausted by how she treated me, and I was prepared to fight her if needed. She slowly moved out of the way and started laughing.

"Go ahead and go to church, Miss Little Perfect! You're not a Christian! Why would God want you!" She spit in anger.

I moved quickly to my car while she continued. Tears rushed to my eyes. Her darts of hatred had hit their mark, and shame came with them. I made sure not to cry until I was far enough from the house she couldn't see me. I wasn't anywhere near perfect, and I never tried to be. I didn't know how to combat the lies that I kept hearing in my head. Was she right that I wasn't a Christian? I knew in my heart I was, but I wasn't sure. I went to the altar several times before Luke and I got married. I even got baptized a few weeks before the ceremony. Honestly, I didn't know enough about being a Christian that I could say beyond any doubt that I was saved. Nothing felt different, and I was seeking God wholeheartedly. These unanswered questions would plague me for most of my adult life. I was a mess when I got to Luke's house, where he was waiting for me. He knew when I stepped out of the car, I was upset. I rushed into his open arms. Several times, he asked what was wrong, but I couldn't say anything other than Mom upset me. I never told him what happened in those moments before I left. He walked me to the passenger side of his truck, opened the door, and let me sit down.

I looked at him and said, "I have to get the rest of my stuff out of my room before the end of the day."

"Okay, we can take care of that when church is over. You don't have much left there, so it shouldn't take long." He said, encouraging me.

He walked around to the other side and got in. I didn't want to go to church in my current state. Luke made me feel safe, and I wanted to be near the comforting peace he gave me. Luke was going to college during this time, but he had come home for the weekend and was helping me move into his parents' house. I was still scared of his mom because she was a force to be reckoned with, but she would never hurt me. Anna was such a stark contrast to my mom. She knew who she was and wasn't afraid to let the truth be heard. Sometimes, the truth hurt, but I grew to love her for it. Keith was a quiet soul that carried so much wisdom. He was the opposite of Anna, but when he spoke, you listened because of the wisdom that he would speak.

I know now where Luke got that from. It was wonderful to be in a place without a need to protect myself, and I started to let my guard down. I learned at Anna's elbow how to run a house and, more importantly, how to cook. She had such a gift, and I was eager to learn. She only had two sons and always hoped for a daughter. I wanted a mother who would love me despite who I was. She did that. She took me under her wing willingly when Luke made his intentions known to his parents. They trusted their son's judgment, even though they probably asked questions about me. I learned about God and the bible from both, and they spoke freely about it. It was an ongoing conversation in the house.

We had five weeks to plan the wedding. It wouldn't have happened, though, without the help of Luke's family. They did everything for us. All I had to do was give ideas and suggestions. This was the first time I had experienced this willingness to jump in and help. This type of giving was unheard of for me. They poured out what they had, as well as their love. This environment was the exact opposite of what I grew up knowing. If you wanted something in my family, there was always a trade-off. I called my grandparents in plenty of time for them to be there. I was turned down and told they wished I wasn't getting married. I needed to get out in the world, make a name for myself, and do something with my life. I was doing something with my life, choosing to be Luke's wife. That was my choice, and it was not theirs.

That was the problem. For my mom to come, I had to take time off work and spend the money I needed to buy her an outfit for the wedding. That was the only way she was coming. Sixty dollars was a lot of money back then when Anna spent $100 on my wedding dress that someone sewed from a drawing I made. Like Luke's family, I wanted my family to share in the celebration with me and give freely. I wanted them to be happy that I was marrying a good man. Not one of them helped but wanted to say what to do. By the time the day came, I was so hurt that I almost let it ruin the day. I had to take time to be by myself. I needed to release a few tears. I had no one to walk me down the aisle when it should have been my grandfather. I had to pay for Mom to be there, with money I could have used to plan the wedding.

I was getting ready, and Anna came to check on me. She was trying to hurry me along and noticed the tears still falling on my cheeks. She didn't ask; she just scooped me up in a huge hug and just held me. It reminded me that I had someone special waiting for me at the church and didn't need to be late. I hurried to get myself ready and slipped on the gown. It was so beautiful. The satin glistened with a bluish hue in the room's light. I hadn't experienced wearing something so lovely before. I stood before the mirror in awe; I was beautiful. That gown made me feel like a diamond in the rough; it held so much promise for days to come. Tears gathered in my eyes, and I blinked them away so my makeup wouldn't run. I just stood there admiring myself in disbelief. My heart wished for things from my family, and my head knew that wouldn't change. I took one last look and a deep breath. I would not let what should have been, ruin one of the best days of my life. I started to the door, and Anna entered the room. She helped me gather up the skirt of the dress, and we hurried out the door.

On the way to the van, it started snowing. Giant snowflakes were everywhere. Seeing snowfall is a favorite of mine. It was like God smiling at me, saying he approved my choice. Time stood still for a moment, and I felt the love of my heavenly Father. It was surreal but frigid in that dress. We got to the church with about an inch on the ground. I waited in the van until it was time for the bridal party to enter the church. The church didn't have a foyer, so I stood outside while everyone else walked down the aisle ahead of me. I waited until it was just me and said a silent prayer to God to calm my nerves and distractions in my head. I thanked Him for Luke and this family I was about to enter. I would take the Harris name proudly.

One last big breath and the door was opened for me, and I was helped in. My skirt was straightened, and everyone turned and looked at me. I glanced at my mom for her approval, and there was none. Then, my eyes found Luke, and everything else faded into the background. I started forward, walking slowly, counting in between steps. My eyes never left him; he was my future. At that moment, I knew that no matter what I faced after this, he would be there for me, and

I for him. We vowed nothing in this world would tear us apart. We would stand shoulder to shoulder and face the pain that my family caused and walk through my healing together. He did not know everything, but I knew he would not run when the shame and hurt came out. The ceremony was a blur, and before I knew it, Luke lifted my veil and engulfed me in a kiss that claimed me as his own. Our reception was beautiful. Everything was expertly prepared for the event. I forgot about everyone there and just enjoyed being in Luke's presence. I struggled to wrap my mind around the reality of being his wife. I loved him more than I thought I could love someone. Every time thought about it, my heart hurt from the fullness of love I felt. I was ready to start this part of my life, no matter what lay ahead. He would help me see past who I thought I was. He led me to know I was so much more. The reception was winding down, so we decided to leave. It was still snowing, so we didn't get far for our first night on the honeymoon. It wouldn't have mattered where we went; I would go along if I was in Luke's presence.

We moved a couple times during the first year of marriage. We both tried going to school and working full-time while trying to build a marriage. It was hard on both of us. I was striving to get past my childhood and tried to navigate things like my family did. I kept shoving down these little things that pricked me about him. I would make the best of it and move on. As you can imagine, I just got full of everything he had done wrong and exploded on him one day. The poor man didn't know what to do. He just sat there reeling as I hurled all these injustices at him.

The problem was he did not remember any of it. I held on to everything. The time, how it made me feel, and what he did. He didn't know what to do at this point other than apologize and try to do better. We agreed on that first blow-up that I needed to come to him when it happened. What he didn't understand was I wasn't used to voicing anything. I didn't know how to open up about my hurt. All I knew was what I watched in my family, which wasn't healthy. Luke would have to be patient with me as I learned healthy argument strategy. So much of my past would come out during these times. I had this notion that my past would fade away as I got away from that time. The problem was it never left like I thought it would. I still carried the burden of my past, but I didn't know how to lay any of it down. It didn't matter how often I went to the altar and pleaded with God. Everything would still come back, sometimes even more potent.

I could not break the chains of my past. I learned how to bear the weight of it and the weight of my new life. I didn't know how to share any of this with Luke because it was just so ugly. I believed the lie that he would leave me if he truly knew what I carried with me. Honestly, there is a lot in my life that I never shared with him until I wrote this book. I never told him because I was desperate to forget it all. So we went on learning how to fight with one another. Learning to listen to each other and working on what was needed.

It wasn't long before the end of that first year I was pregnant with our first son, Jacob. Those pregnancy hormones are no joke. They had me all over the place. There were times that I didn't recognize the person who would jump out in the most inopportune times. Mostly while driving/riding in the car. Luke didn't know what to do with all the emotion, and neither did I. It was also during this time that I was trying to grow a relationship with my mom. Mom needed to open a checking account. She needed a safe place to deposit money while she traveled with a new guy she found, and I believed her.

Mom was faithful for a time at putting money in the account and saving much of it. Then, one day, it was all gone, and she was still writing checks. The bank started taking money from my and Luke's accounts to make everything even. That wasn't going to happen! We needed every penny we had to live. I called her to discuss the problem that she needed to get money back into the account. I also told her the bank took money from my account to cover it. She denied everything, and the innocent phone call to discover what was happening turned into a shouting match about me, never doing enough to help her. She said she would not add more money to cover the overdrafts.

I was devastated, reeling from the shock of something so outrageous. I was dumbfounded. Luke asked what happened, and he got a look of anger. That was his money, too. He worked hard for it, and it was supposed to go to us, not her. That day, we went to the bank and closed that account because we couldn't close the other because it was overdrafted. I had trusted her to do the right thing, but she stole from us. Because of her, it took me forever to open a bank account in my name after that. The amount I would have to pay back to clear my name was not something we could handle then. I wasn't going to pay for a mistake she willingly made either. We had been trying to save what little we had to prepare for the baby, and now it was gone. I felt so much shame for what Mom did to us. I was so desperate for a relationship with her. I was naive to think she wouldn't do something like this. If it hadn't been for Luke's family and their friends, I don't know how we would have gotten what was needed for Jacob and his arrival. I don't know if Luke told them what happened, but they stepped up and did what needed to be done. Yet I continued to let this woman back into my life repeatedly. Forgiving and trying to forget what she had done. My family would contact me and tell me that I needed to forgive her and let her back in. As a good girl, I would do what they asked; I would always be a good girl. Defeated is more of what I felt. I wasn't good unless I made them happy. My mental welfare wasn't a concern to them. That should have stopped me long ago, but it didn't. This toxic cycle continued for years.

Anna stayed with us when Jacob was born to help care for him. I had to have a C-section because he was breached and losing amniotic fluid. He was in distress before his birth. Most of Luke's family showed up for his arrival. He was so loved. As much love was in that room, I longed for my mom to walk through the door. I wanted her to see her first grandson. She never showed, even though I had begged her to be there. So, as I watched Luke's family with our son, my heart hurt that she never showed up. I was crying, but it wasn't because I was happy, despite putting on a good face. I was very happy, but she ruined it for me.

I had the privilege of becoming a stay-at-home mom in this season of raising children. Luke did what he had to do to ensure we were provided for. At times, he worked 3 different jobs to cover everything. It was hard at times, but I don't remember suffering much. Everything was covered, and we always had a little extra. As Jacob grew, I started to think about my childhood, and fear crept in on the mother I wanted to become. I even started having dreams of the things I went through happening to him. Could I be the mother that my children would need? Could I rise above my past and do better? I didn't have any answers. Deep in my heart, I knew I wanted to be for them what I didn't get as a child. That was my heart cry and what propelled me forward for the children God would bless me with. I knew with everything in my being, my children would never suffer the injustices I had. They would never know the pain of that.

The pregnancy with Grace came shortly after Jacob was born, and we were moving closer to Luke's parents and home. I wanted horses again. Luke asked his dad if I could put a couple in his fields. He didn't like horses but tolerated it if they didn't chase his cattle. I asked my mom if it would be possible for me to have the horses I worked so hard with in high school. After all, in my mind, I had a right to them. After all, she called them mine while working with them. I don't remember how everything happened, but she blew up and said I was trying to take something for nothing. And I'm sure I didn't respond in the right frame of mind, either. However, at the end of it all, I was disowned by her. What in the world? How did I get here? I was just speechless. This was over horses? All I wanted was horses, and somehow I got disowned? She hung up on me, not that I could say anything anyway; I was dumbstruck. I remember now. It seemed so rehearsed. This felt like something she had hidden in her back pocket. She had been waiting for the right moment to spring that on me.

I did nothing to deserve her treating me like that. I was angry, hurt, and disbelieving any of it. I sat there in a daze until Jacob's cries pulled me back from my pain. I went and picked him up, looking at his angry little face. Tears poured down my face. How could a mother do that to her child? I could not imagine doing something like that to someone so precious. I changed his diaper and fed him, crying my pain out at the same time. I looked over at my precious boy, trying to sort through the pain that I had been dealt. He looked up at me while feeding himself to notice the pain on my face. He stopped what he was doing and reached for me.

"Mama, hug?" he said, his chubby little arms outstretched.

I let him embrace me, and I cried on his tiny shoulder. I needed someone to hold me, and God used my sweet son. I can't tell you how many times God used my children to calm the storms that my mother caused. As I think now, nothing my children can do will ever make me do something like this. My relationship with them means more to me than what they can do wrong. Their relationship with me is close to my heart. It will be protected there no matter what. Something as stupid as asking for horses would never make me sever ties with them.

We moved home, and this was a time of struggle. We were barely able to make ends meet. We had a car repossessed because we just couldn't cover the payment. It was choosing between food on the table or a car to drive. We started attending church regularly, seeking God and asking him to provide. Yet again, Luke's mom and dad stepped up and helped where they could, giving what they had. I was so thankful they always helped, even if they did without. They let us live in a home they built to sell because we had no other options. This is when they became Mom and Dad to me. Even though I had the pain of being disowned, it didn't give me the sorrow it should have. I grew into the woman I wanted to become without my mom's influence. My grandmother begged me to forgive her several times, and I explained that she disowned me. The truth was, I had forgiven her. She was the one who removed me from her life, and I was strangely okay with that.

I gave birth to Grace that spring by another C-section. I woke up in the night with contractions and thought they were gas pains. Trust me, I had some awful gas pains with my babies. I sat on the toilet, hoping that the pain would pass, but it didn't. I called Anna because Luke was four hours away from home working. She and Keith showed up. She helped me into the van and asked how far apart the contractions were. I didn't realize that's what they were. By the time we got to the hospital, they were 5 minutes apart. My body was gearing up to start pushing by the time they got me to the operating room. I was supposed to have a normal birth after the first one. But some old doctor at the group office I was visiting vowed I was going to rupture, and I and the baby could die. I had already had one C-section, so what was another. They had me in the operating room and were trying to get the epidural in, and I couldn't curl far enough forward. Do you know how hard it is to curl forward, being 9 months pregnant? It's impossible! I was contracting on top of that. I was praying they would get it where it needed to be soon.

I knew once it was in, my whole body would relax. Thank you, God! They helped me lay down on the table. They set up the surgery, and I thought I was going to be alone in there. Nope, they brought my mother-in-law in. Yep, she saw everything and especially loved watching the surgery. Soon, Grace was born, and we both were crying.

## Adulthood: Overcoming My Childhood

As much as I wished for Luke to be there, sharing that with her was precious. Watching her enjoy the moment her granddaughter was being born. This was my greatest gift to the woman who gave me love without question. Luke would be there soon, and we could all enjoy it together.

Sorrow crept into my heart during that, though. Oh, how I wished I had a mother that loved me as much as Anna did. To grow up in the love and acceptance of someone like her would have meant so much. How much different would I be if I had got that? I had to blink back the tears because now was not the time to cry with sadness. After post-op, the nurses helped me to my room. As I entered the room, Luke was standing, holding his daughter, whispering to her. It was such a beautiful sight, and that memory of that split second before he realized I was coming into the room is one I will remember forever.

With Jacob, everything was rushed and unprepared. My post-op took a while to recover from. I had missed this moment between Luke and Jacob. Remembering that sight still catches my breath. He was standing next to the window, the morning sun filtering through and casting light on the scene. His tiny daughter bundled up in a pink blanket. She was in his arms, bouncing gently, talking to her softly. The look of love on his face for his child, slight smile, proudness of what he helped create. Then, the love he showed me as I entered the room. I reached for both; the scene was so precious. Anna had gone home for a while, so it was just us in the room. I needed rest, and Luke took care of Grace. I closed my eyes and let the scene play repeatedly in my mind as I drifted off to sleep. During the year and the troubles we had faced through it, this moment made it all fade.

Luke moved us shortly after Grace was born. We did not like being apart. During this time, we moved every little bit because one job would end, and we would be on to the next. One day, out of the blue, my grandmother called me and told me I needed to forgive my mom and let her back in. She told me how forgiveness is good for the soul and how lonely my mom was. With new found confidence, I tried to explain to her that I didn't cause this. I wasn't the one that was disowned. If Mom wanted a relationship with me, she would have to come back to me. However, Grandma wouldn't hear it and ended the conversation with, "It would make me very happy if you would do it for me." I felt defeated at that moment. I respected my grandmother, but I wasn't sure I wanted my mother back in my life. I had forgiven her, but my life was good now. I was growing and thriving in our little family. My grandma reminded me that Mom needed to be part of my kids' lives. I wasn't sure I wanted that either, with how she treated me. I felt terrible in my heart that my mom was lonely. I agonized over this decision, and none of it felt like the right choice. If I refused to let her back in, Grandma would be angry. If I let Mom back into my life, would she change how she acted? I didn't want any more episodes that started all of this. It wasn't worth it anymore to me.

I gave in and called Mom to keep Grandma happy, even though I was unsure of everything. I called Mom, I apologized, and I forgave her. In the process, everything was blamed on me all in one conversation. Mom never apologized for what she did. It was almost like she tattled on me to Grandma. She even blamed me for the disowning and said I was the one that disowned her. What was I doing? I should have just let what Grandma said go. But again, no one cares about what I want. If I do what's best for me, then I'm selfish.

I never understood the mentality of my family. Keep Mom or Grandma happy, and everyone is okay. That takes no one else into consideration. But here I was; Mom was back in my life, and I had to deal with it. From then on, I kept her at a distance that I thought she could do little damage. Mom didn't understand why I wouldn't let her closer. She was the reason why. We moved a lot during this time, so she didn't come and visit. I just had to put up with the occasional phone call of her talking about all the animals she had. She rarely wanted to talk about something other than herself and her stuff. I would just sit there on the phone, saying yes, no, and Mom, I must go; the kids need me. She would huff and say goodbye. Occasionally, she would ask how we were doing.

Mom would listen long enough to halfway hear and then move on to the next thing she wanted to talk about. She would also always complain that I never called her. This was how it went for many years until social media emerged. I started messaging her instead of calling because I had what had been said in black and white. She would not be able to twist my words any longer. She broke so many things when she disowned me that she never owned up to. Yet she expected the relationship to go back better than it was before. Due to previous years of hurt from this woman, I could no longer let her close.

We moved around for a couple of years, moving with the jobs. It was an adventure for us as a family but also hard. I had boxes in the closet that never got unpacked and empty ones to fill, to move at a moment's notice. The money was good, and Luke was in his element. If anyone ever had a gift and knowledge for building, it was Luke. He could look at these problems presented to him and figure out a way to get from point A to point B. As much as he loved it, it wore on him. The hours were long, the work hard, and often hot. We never went anywhere cool, just the hot south. The kids were getting older. We missed home and being around his family. They missed us, too. We had a difficult decision to make. If we moved home, he would have to find a job supporting us, which is problematic in the middle of nowhere. Or we continue to be on the road and make this our life. I knew what I wanted because I hated moving. I had done it my whole life and only wanted to continue doing it if we bought a camper. I was fine with that because the money was good, and Luke loved his work. However, we would have to homeschool the kids. Being up to that task left me uncertain. Luckily, he decided that he wanted to go home as well. We moved into a mobile home next to where his grandfather lived. Everything in this valley was what I was searching for.

Granted, we would eventually have to build a house, but that would come when it was meant to. For the first time, I felt God saying to me welcome home. Everything wasn't as I wanted, but I wasn't moving anymore. No more packing or wondering where the next place was going to be. We would be near family for holidays and birthdays. This place would go a long way to help me heal from the trauma that I went through. The solace of the nature surrounding me was soothing, complete with a creek and a large yard. This was the place that I needed desperately to sink roots into, a solid place.

It wasn't long before we settled in that I longed for another child. I loved my kids and wanted a house full. This child would be bittersweet, though. After this pregnancy, I couldn't have any more. With two other C-sections, it would become dangerous for me to carry any more children because of the likelihood of my uterus tearing. Luke was fine with the two we had but eventually gave in to my pleas. Side story: I had to be on birth control for most of our marriage to this point because we were a fertile combination. God must have heard my pleas for another child because I got pregnant while on birth control. I had to laugh because whether Luke wanted another child or not, it was too late now. Soon after the realization, I began to cry almost every day. This would be my last; no more children will be after this. There would be no more growing the baby and feeling the first flutters of movement. No more anticipation of them being born. No more sweet newborn baby smell. This was the last time I would experience those things personally as a mother.

I was working on the time on the farm with Luke, and something very unexpected happened. I remember standing in one of the buildings, preparing for the day. As I was standing there, my lower back was hurting, slowing the progress of what I was doing. Before long, I felt a big gush of fluid between my legs. My breath caught, and I teared up. None of this ever happened with the other pregnancies. I knew something was very wrong. Trying to hold myself together, I went in search of Luke. I needed to get to the doctor quickly. I passed Anna on the way out of the door. She knew something was wrong. I only got out "baby" and "something is wrong" before I rushed through the door. We both started yelling for Luke. Luke came rushing down the hill, worry on his face.

"What's wrong?" he said in between breaths.

"Amanda needs to get to the doctor; something is wrong with the baby!" Anna said for me.

I was thankful she was there. I couldn't bring myself to speak. Anna had experienced the loss of a child. So, she held me tight while Luke ran to get his truck.

"It's going to be alright. It happens to the best of us." She said as she tried to soothe me.

I could just nod my head through the tears. I didn't want to be one of the ones. I wanted this baby, my baby, to live. She stood there holding me until Luke pulled up. He took me home to change the pants that were soaked in fluid and blood. My heart was so broken; how could this have happened. Cleaned up, we got in his truck and headed to the doctor's office. Of all the pain I had experienced, nothing came close to the thought of losing a child. I just sat there numbly while tears fell, praying God wouldn't take my baby. Luke tried to encourage and console me. I didn't hear any of it. All I could hear was my sorrow at the news coming and the pleas that I was praying. The wait to see the doctor seemed to last forever. Sitting there, I continued to cry despite the stares I received from everyone. I didn't care what I looked like; I was losing a child! Social graces were the furthest thing from my mind. I felt like a black hole was threatening to swallow me.

I didn't even hear the nurse call my name. Luke reached for me, and I came around. I prayed silently as we walked through the hallway to the exam room. We went through the preliminary exam. I was barely able to tell them what was going on. Then, the nurse got down in my line of sight.

"Amanda, don't assume the worst right now. Let us see what is happening, and then we can form those thoughts afterward. There is so much that can happen that is not the worst. So, we will move you to the ultrasound room and examine the baby. Okay?" she said in a calm voice.

I nodded. Luke was there with me in those moments, but I felt alone. I was hoping for the best and preparing for the worst. They took me to the other room and sat me on the table. Luke sat next to me, holding my hand. He was worried, too, but I didn't know how to comfort him then. The nurse got everything prepped and began the ultrasound. It was so silent you could hear a pin drop in that room. I was watching her face for any indication of what had happened; there wasn't any. The ultrasound wasn't making any sounds, and I couldn't tell what she was looking at; I was only 2 months along.

She got a puzzled look on her face, "Well, it would be helpful if the sound was turned up. There, that's better!"

The sound that was coming out of the machine was the sweetest sound I had ever heard in my life. It was a heartbeat. There was something different about it, though it almost had an echo.

"Well, now that we can hear them. Here's baby number one and baby number two. Everything is fine." She said plainly.

I missed that part because of my sheer relief, but Luke didn't.

"Excuse me, say that again!" Luke still not fully understanding what she said.

"Okay, there's two babies. Didn't you know that?" she asked.

I entered the conversation, "Well, no, we are waiting for our first appointment."

In all his practicalness, Luke blurted, "That explorer is not going to work!"

We didn't have a family vehicle then because the engine went out in what we had, and we were borrowing Anna's van. We tried several places to get a car, but nothing worked. I love when God reveals his answers all at once.

I looked at the nurse and said, "What was that fluid?"

"The best I can tell is that a large watery cyst ruptured. They are sort of common, but you are in no danger. I would take it easy to de-stress for the next couple of days, but you can resume normal activities after that." She informed.

"Thank you," I said.

"I am going to slip outside and let you get dressed." The nurse said quietly with a smile.

I sat up in a daze. Did that just really happen? I came here expecting to lose the one baby I had, just to find out there were two. How was that possible? Luke helped me off the table, both of us too stunned to speak. I got dressed, and we stepped into the hall. I felt like I was in a daze, emotionally spent because I thought I was going to lose the baby. Only to find out there were two, and they were healthy? Now I was crying again because how would I take care of two? I just started laughing. I felt like I was losing my mind. We got back in the truck, and I glanced at Luke. He was shell-shocked. He just looked at me, and we both started rejoicing. God had answered our prayers and gave us two babies instead of one. He had also given me more than 3, and I was grateful. We got back to Luke's mom and dad, and a bunch of people were waiting for us to share the news. They were there to comfort us because, at that moment, they thought we had lost the baby. It turned into a party because they learned that I was still pregnant and I had twins. This is what I learned about Luke's family. They pulled together no matter what. In joy and in sorrow, they were there. To this day, I thank God for those people and how they showed me the way a family should be. Love and acceptance are what they showed.

Not the condemnation I grew up knowing. I grew tired from the day's events and asked Luke to take me home so I could lie down. He ensured I was fine when he dropped me off and returned to spend time with the family. The quietness of the house would let me sleep. Before I got into bed, I felt a stirring to call my mom. At this point in my life, our relationship was not bad. I called and told her the events of the day. She was upset that I didn't call her before going to the doctor's office. I explained that there wasn't time. The only reason Anna knew was because she was there when everything happened. She mumbled something about me always going to Anna first.

I said, "Mom!" sternly, trying to get her to focus on something other than my relationship with my mother-in-law.

"I'm trying to tell you what happened," I continued.

"Well, did you lose the baby?" she asked bluntly.

I stopped in my telling of the situation and realized she didn't care. But I was still trying to build a relationship with her because she was my mom, so I continued.

"No, actually, I am pregnant with twins." I ended.

There was silence on the other end. Then, she revealed a concise history lesson about my family. Grandma and her both had been pregnant with twins and lost them. I started to ask what happened, but she cut me short. She didn't have much faith that I would carry them full term. Those words cut deep. Thanks for the vote of confidence. We said our goodbyes. Tears slipped down my face. Just once, I wanted her happy for me; just once, I wanted her to say well done. I started to pray. Those thoughts of losing my precious babies would

## Adulthood: Overcoming My Childhood

have to go. If there was one thing about me, I wouldn't give up without a fight. What had happened in the past was the past. I had to look forward. I laid down on the bed and pleaded with God to help me get through this pregnancy. I slept that afternoon, resting in the peace that God would get me through this.

I prayed almost every day for my womb to stay healthy and that my body would protect those little ones that God gave me to carry. Good on His word; God helped me through. The carrying of twins was hard on every part of my body. Not to mention the amount of food I had to eat and the sleepless nights. One of them liked moving all day and the other all night. I rested as much as possible with two other little ones running around. Luke helped where he could, but he worked on the farm full-time. In the dead of winter, Faith and Noah were born at term. Both were fully grown and weighed the amounts of normal babies. Together, they weighed almost fifteen pounds. Everyone came to see the twins in the hospital and the first few days at home. Everyone but my mom. I know that this is the wrong thinking, but I wanted to look her in the eye and say that I did it. That my body triumphed where her's didn't.

The truth was God made it so; he made me strong through this despite what she had said. My relationship had changed with God during that time. He gave me a good model of what being a parent looks like. Children are precious in His sight. Relationships are a top priority to Him. Raising children to be independent, guiding and directing them is not for the fainthearted. Jacob is a strong-willed, highly intelligent person who always questions the boundaries that we set. He would always step foot over and then start testing them for weaknesses. He was always ready to give me a hug if needed. Jacob also had a learning disability and struggled through school. It was heartbreaking at times, but he got through it. Grace was and still is my happiest child; she almost always smiles and makes little noises as she moves about her day, making her endearing. Grace is also a "to the letter" person and often is very hard on herself when she needs to be. She is very outspoken and can take charge even when I don't need her to. Faith is my mini-me in every way. She is smart, driven, and has a great wit. She is a great thinker, and always hungers for knowledge. She is quiet, though, and doesn't speak up for herself. Often, people will run her over with their words. Noah is my light on a cloudy day child. He always makes me laugh. He has a kind, compassionate heart and gives freely to others. Noah was also diagnosed with SVT (Supraventricular tachycardia). He must be careful what he does so it doesn't set his heart off. His sharp wit also comes with a sharp tongue that must often be kept in check.

I know all this because I have developed a relationship with my children. They got me through some tough times in life. Overcoming what I went through as a child helped to shape what I would become as a parent. We allowed our children to speak their truths openly. We always kept the lines of communication open and taught them that it was okay to come to us when they had trouble. Nothing is more humbling as a parent when your child openly points out what needs to change in you as a parent. That was sometimes a hard pill to swallow. That is what it is like. Building and keeping a relationship with someone you love. It's always constantly evolving and changing. Hearing and accepting our children made us the parents we are today. I can say with utmost assurance that it is because of God and them that I am the parent I am today. That became one of my greatest triumphs. I know I didn't write many stories about my children, but I feel like those are their stories to tell, even though I took part in them. We have been through many ups and downs as a family. A lot of what we went through is personal to them and me. That is except what God has wanted me to put in this book. I look forward with great joy to who my children are becoming. I will be their biggest cheerleader with their accomplishments. I will also be there for them when they need a shoulder to cry on. My children are leaving the nest, but I know that God has them in the palm of His hand. After all, they are his children entirely.

## Pivot Point:

Looking back through these years of adulthood, I saw how blessed I was. Did I have trouble? Yes, that is one thing that is assured in life. I overcame so much with God's help. When I stood on the edge of adulthood, I was so scared of becoming like my mom. As much as I hate to say, part of me did become her. Some of it is good, but some of it is bad. It is a constant fight to keep that side of me under control. It is so ingrained into who I am as a person.

> "We can make our plans, but the Lord determines the steps." **Proverbs 16:9**

God took what little I had in adulthood and turned it into much more. I became to my children the person I needed when I was a child. To my husband, I became his best friend, and it has been my honor to walk beside him for the last 25 years. God knew what He was doing when he put us together. Some of the best parts of myself have come out because God was and still is working on me. One assurance is that God has plans for me in my life, and while I still don't know what they all are, He will continue to guide and direct me.

# CHAPTER 7

# Restoration: My Testimony

**THIS IS MY** story. I know that I went through things that people would not understand. I also believe that I was allowed to experience pain, hurt, rejection, fear, anxiety, and so many other things because that would allow me to connect with others on a personal level. I know that you are reading that statement asking why a good God would allow something like this to happen to an innocent child? This honestly is a question that I have asked many times myself. It all comes down to this, free will. God is a loving father and a gentleman. He will not push himself on you, demanding you to listen to him. God will not force you to love him. He does not want his creation to be robots. He gives us the freedom to make our own choices. The choices we make are the direction that our lives will go.

I realized that God had me in His hands this whole time. Every step, every moment, he held me, feeling my pain. God was holding my hand, guiding me forward, carrying me if needed. Looking back, I can see how often he intervened on my behalf. Helping me hide, leaving the hole in the wall of that one house, blocking the door, and keeping danger from me when I was alone. All these reasons pointed me toward Jesus and healing. Unless I missed my guess, you have a reason for picking up this book. Are you searching for answers or healing? Could it be that you wanted to know that someone else understands the gut-wrenching pain you have been through? Whatever the reason,

I want you to realize that I know, and more importantly, God knows. So, I want to give you one last look at my life and the events that led me to move forward with healing.

I sat up on the edge of the bed, trying to convince myself that I could go to work and everything would be fine. I tried to pull strength from my body and had little left. How did I get here? I did not know how to put one foot in front of the other anymore. I just wanted to lie back down, close my eyes, and forget about the world. I did not know who I was. I listened to what everyone else had told me to be for years leading up to this. When I asked myself who I was, all I heard was their voices. Not mine and definitely not God's. I had a relationship with Him, but what I wanted between us still seemed unattainable. I felt like I needed this magical key to unlock what only the chosen could find.

Don't get me wrong, I was a good Christian woman! At least, that is what I told myself. I taught Sunday school classes, led worship, was involved in life groups, and am an elder's wife. Still, something was missing, something was wrong. I felt like I was looking through a foggy, scratched lens that I could never get clean enough to see through. Luke never failed to stand by me as I pushed myself to be the best I could be. He tried to keep me from running myself into the ground. I could not let go of the need for approval. The need to hear my mom say I'm proud of you. The need to hear my grandmother say what a wonderful woman you have become. Sadly, I probably would never hear those words, and I took my identity from that.

This realization hit me when I was recovering from COVID. Mom insisted that she was going to come and stay with us. She did not hear my pleas to ask her to stay home. Luke had to call her back and tell her she didn't need to come. I was really sick. Even then, she pushed to come. She did not hear anything that was said. She only listened to her wants and her needs. It took her husband to say no before she agreed, and even then, she tried to change his mind. My children could see how much she had hurt me and how strained the relationship was. They also knew how little she gave to them. They didn't have much of a relationship with her and did not want one. Grace even went as far as to say that she didn't want Grandma Nancy at her LPN pinning ceremony. This was a big moment for Grace. She knew the trouble that my mom would cause. Mom had to be center stage with all attention on her. She did this when Grace and Jacob graduated and would do it again. Nothing my mom did earned a place of position in my children's hearts. Mom wanted respect for the position but did nothing to earn it.

The truth was, I did not want her in my life anymore. I was fatigued by the roller coaster ride she always sent me on. We would be okay one minute. The next minute, I did something horribly and utterly wrong. I was tired of trying to please her and never knowing how to do it. It seemed like it was never enough, and I was exhausted. It took my children seeing things about them on her social media to seal the tomb for me. You can say or do anything about me, but don't you dare cross that line with my children. And that's a line that she crossed. I walked away, and she had no idea why. If I responded, she would never own up to what was said and feign innocence. If approached, she would turn my words on me or against my children, claiming they lied to me. I saw the comments in black and white for myself, and my children rarely lied to me. I did not want to play her game anymore.

To top everything off, I fell into depression after this. I should have been relieved or elated that I let something so heavy go, but I wasn't. Everything I had been striving for was for her, for her approval. I didn't have that driving force; I felt I had nothing. I didn't realize how overwhelmed and burnt out I was. Years of carrying that need for approval had got me nowhere. All this time, I thought I needed that. Now, I wonder why I put myself through all the struggles. Looking back now, I should have listened to Luke and his wisdom. He wanted me to find what I wanted, but I could not let it go. I would let that little girl down inside me if I did that. The person I should have been caring about should have been me. How could Luke and my children see something I didn't?

All those years ago, when I was disowned, my family wanted me to be the one to mend the relationship. Nobody once asked for my side of the story or how I was abused. Now, I was an outcast. A black sheep is what I am called. I was shamed for wanting more in my life. No one wanted my side of the story, only that I needed to fix the problem. If I did not step away from her, I would never heal the wounds that she always cut back open. All the years after Tony died, they did not ask about my childhood. If my family truly cared, they would have asked. No, they only wanted peace and happiness for themselves, no matter how it came. They wanted me to swallow all the offenses and move on. I had grown tired of swallowing everything they fed me.

My life, health, and even marriage had reached the limit of what they could stand. I knew Luke was tired of picking me back up whenever they knocked me down. He was tired of placing band-aids on the gaping wounds they would leave in their wake. Nothing ever genuinely healed from my childhood, either. I thought that just getting away from that situation, time would eventually heal them. The wounds were more infected than I realized through all of this. Those wounds kept getting ripped open by the same people who put them there, and I allowed it. I allowed them to continuously hurt me for the sake of maintaining the relationship. I had to walk away. It was painful but necessary. At first, I was constantly reminded that she was my mom or they were my family. Or that I needed to give them another chance. I was all out of second chances. This came from people who did not have to live in the shadow of my family. They came from loving homes that loved and cared for one another. The stark reality was I didn't. For my healing, I had to let go and move on.

The first few steps away from them were some of the hardest I have ever taken. The chains and bondage of these relationships were familiar. I was rejected more times than I could count. But I didn't let it harden my heart. Even with the rejection, I allowed them to pull at me. I desperately wanted freedom. God gave me reassurance that I did the right thing. The thought of letting go of them scared me. I could not picture my life without the ones that caused the trauma in it. Being an over-thinker by nature, entirely relying on God, seemed unfathomable. Every one of His steps were precisely measured and my were erratically misguided. It was an uncomfortable and unexpected place for me to be.

The pressure to remain would be unbearable at times. I was so afraid that I would go backward and return to what I knew. The toxicity of my past called to me, offering comfort and familiarity. Something rose up in me that was undeniable. It reminded me that my past was nothing but hurts and fears. It kept asking, "What if." What if you continue to push through? What if you fully trust God and His ways, not your own? What if this changes the course of your life? And the questions continued still until reason set in. My past and my control of it was always what I had done. Yes, it was familiar, but I always encountered the same situations. Nothing changed, nothing moving forward. I wanted different, and I certainly wanted off this perpetual hamster wheel.

Sometimes, the fact that I don't have any family from my past is heart-wrenching. I still want them. I just don't want them in their current state, though. I want to see them healed first. God brought me to my knees over this. He was very loud in my head, tenderly saying that He was everything I needed. I needed to heal but did not know how to ask for it. I fought to return to a place where I could trust people again. I fought to be able to forgive these people who cut me to my very core. I forgave my Dad for all the horrendous things that he did to me when my Mom thought that it was stupid to do so. To forgive Mom for not loving me or believing me when I said I was being abused. To forgive her over and over when she broke my heart. To forgive myself and allow the pain to never heal. I had to let go of my vision of my family ever being the people I needed them to be. I felt like an orphan and did not understand who God really could be in my life. I did not know how good God really was. I had always viewed him through the lens of the people that raised me. I still didn't understand him as a father. I served him because that's what I thought Christians did, selfless serving and giving, always doing the Lord's work.

My serving was mindless, and I was going through the motions. It was just another thing on the to-do list. I was trying to find the combination to unlock the blessings God had for me. I was people-pleasing my way into God's kingdom and tired. Deep in my soul, I was hurting, screaming for something more. There had to be more! It seemed beyond my comprehension of who God really was. I wanted to compare my relationship with my earthly parents to Him, and you cannot do that. Even with good parents, it's still impossible. Soon, I would start to learn who He was.

Mark 5:25 is a story about a woman with an issue of blood. She had this issue for 12 years and suffered at the hands of many doctors. Because of this issue, she was isolated from everyone and was considered unclean. She was not allowed personal connection with anyone because they would become a part of her problem and become unclean as well. She had lost trust and hope in people and what they could do for her. She had heard about Jesus and the miracles that he had done. He always had a crowd of people around him. How was she going to get to him and let him heal her? She reasoned that she would have to slip through the crowd and touch the hem of his garment. This was the one portion of his robe she could touch, and he would not be considered unclean.

She kept telling herself, "If I could just touch his hem, I would be healed.

Faith propelled her through the crowd, and she could touch him without him noticing, or so she thought. Jesus felt the power leave him immediately, and all progression of the crowd stopped. He turned around, scanning the crowd, looking for the one who touched him.

Turning to the disciples, he questioned again, "Who touched me?"

His disciples said, "What are you talking about? With this crowd pushing and jostling you, you're asking, 'Who touched me?' Dozens have touched you!"

Jesus kept on asking, looking for the person responsible.

Fearfully, The woman stepped forward and said, "I touched you, Rabbi." She knelt before him and shared her story.

Jesus kneeled before her, saying, "Daughter, you took the risk of faith, and now you're healed and whole. Live well, and live blessed! Be healed of your plague."

This story always cut through my heart. While I did not have an issue with blood, I could identify with this woman's longing to be whole again and the desire to be loved. Hearing someone say, "Daughter, you are loved and accepted, no strings attached. I have desperately searched for this type of love my entire life. To be loved and have nothing leveraged against it. To be held in the arms of my Father and know that he felt nothing but genuine, honest love for me. By reaching out to him and asking for healing, restoration was about to take full effect in my life, and I wanted it.

Restoration is the action of returning something to a former owner, place, or condition. In construction, you take a building and remove or tear out anything that is damaged, rotting, or not working. It is often getting down to the bare bones of a structure and rebuilding. This is

## Restoration: My Testimony

what God was going to do with me. He would have to remove anything damaged, rotting, or not working. He had his work cut out with me. This process would be slow, but over time, the result would be beautiful. Repairing the broken parts of me would be a painstaking procedure.

I was broken beyond what any person should be able to handle. By continuously standing back up with every hit, I had callouses and rough edges that would have to be made smooth. With my wounds, He would have to remove all the dead, decaying spots to ensure they would heal. He would have to dig all the hatred and resentment up by the roots that caused my continued pain. He wanted me to be able to look at his creation in the mirror and consider how beautiful she had become. He reminded me how intelligent I was by the degrees I had in my name. He ensured I would no longer be that little girl who was always scared and wanted to please everyone. Instead, he would replace her with the original joy I had carried before I witnessed the pain. He would help me find a way to heal and do what it was intended to do. This way, I would pull out all the trauma that kept me in a compromised mental state.

Writing this book was a way that I found my healing. I did not seek any professional guidance for my healing. Though I did not receive professional counseling, I started my healing journey at a women's conference. All it took was a powerful woman of Christ to touch me and tell me that I had some things that I needed to let go of. Pray about the people that God would place in your life that could guide you through this time. Counseling is not wrong by any means, but I could not open myself up to it. Every time I thought about counseling, that voice in my head would remind me, "What happens in this house stays in this house." It was difficult to even share everything from my past with Luke. He did not know the full extent of what I went through until I wrote most of this book.

Still, those events had to come out. 41 years of carrying weight and all the shame that came with it was so heavy. I did not intend for what I wrote to become a book. God had other plans because, while writing, I felt my spirit say that this book would help so many people. I remember it precisely, I was writing, and the thoughts were fluidly coming, and then a whisper came. Several emotions rushed to the surface with the idea. Could I really publish this? Could my story make a difference in others' lives? Then, one thought came to me that still haunts me. If this is published, there's no turning back. What happened during my childhood and adulthood would be in the world for all to see. It would be available for everyone to read, even those that caused the scars. If this book was released, there would be no turning back. That singular thought almost tore me in two. So many questions rushed to the forefront of my mind. Yet this hope sprung up in me. I clung to it with all my strength. What if this brought them healing, too? What if this exposure forced them to look at their lives differently?

I had to take that chance. I placed this in the only hands I knew could take it and make it turn out for good, God's. He would use my sacrifice of openly writing about my past and doing something amazing with it. I could not deny that I wanted to be a part of that, even if it meant that I would lose my family for good. This urgency to complete this task compelled me to continue writing, even when all I could do was sob while telling it. I desperately wanted people like me to learn about the healing that I had received. To hide this would be an injustice to God and what he formed in me. I knew I was on the edge of birthing what I needed to become my entire life. It was painstaking, and some days hurt beyond what I thought was imaginable. It had to happen. It had to come to this for me to finally move on with my life and become the woman I was created to be.

Now my question to you is, what are you going to do? Will you let the words of this book and the truths I share pass you by? Or will you reach out and grab a hold of Jesus with both hands and let him heal you? The choice is yours. I hope you choose the latter. However, it may not be time for you yet. It took me most of my adult life to see where I needed to be, too. In either case, I would like to dispel some of the lies that you are probably hearing in your head right now:

~ You are protected. There is nothing that the love of God cannot cover. He will wrap you in his mighty arms and give you the protective covering you need to feel protected even if you are still in the circumstance that you have fear of. He will make a way where there seems to be no way.

~ You are loved without question. Despite what you have been told in this life, you are loved. God will move heaven and earth to show you his love. He does not want us to suffer in the pain of the events that happened to us. His love is unconditional, with no other motives attached. Let that sink in, and allow his love to cover you.

~ You have a Good Father. If you experienced pain from your parents, it's hard to see a parental figure without seeing through that pain. God is a good father. He does not hold back when giving you what you need. He always goes above and beyond when we have needs we cannot fulfill ourselves.

~ He is proud of you. As hard as it seems, God is proud of you. He sees you. God knows the life you have had. He does not shame you for it. You bring honor to Him. He knows the striving that you have done. He is still proud of you despite all the right or wrong turns. He has the artwork of your life on his refrigerator and proudly points it out to all who will listen.

- You have an ever-faithful friend. If there was anyone that you could talk to, it is Him. Even though he saw it all, he wants to hear about your day in great detail. He longs to listen to your voice, to know your dreams and what excites you about the future. He wants a relationship with you. He wants to be that friend that you run to with everything.

- You are enough. God knows who he made when He created you. He knows who you would be and where you would go. You are not a mistake or an accident. You will always be enough to him. Do not let what the world says about you overshadow what God says. You are everything that you need to be. You are enough.

- You are beautiful. God looked at you in your mother's womb and hand-picked everything about you, from the hairs on your head to the tips of your toes. He handcrafted your DNA into something no one else in this world has. He always revels in his creation, and you are part of that.

- You are smart. With the amount of intelligence that you have, there are no limits. God gave that intelligence so that you can overcome anything that is placed in your way. You are a problem solver and a great thinker. With the intelligence God gave you, there is nothing that you cannot accomplish.

- You are important. You will never be a burden to God. You will never be too much for Him to handle. God looks at you every day to ensure that you are doing well. He is there at every event in your life and will continue to do so until you depart from this world.

I hope you will allow these truths about yourself and God to permeate your thoughts, soul, and heart. These are the truths that I learned while I experienced healing. It is my prayer for you that you will allow healing to come. Even if you don't make that choice now, please give yourself the grace to someday heal. I fully understand what I am asking. I know the ugly that can come out and the pain with it. Some days, it so debilitating that all I could do was sleep and cry. Being on the other side of it, though, is indescribable. The hope and joy that flows through me is something I haven't felt in my life. I still have areas I am working on, but they are much easier to deal with now. I feel so much love from my Father, knowing I have the relationship I want and need with Him. This is the reason why I urge you to pursue healing. Pursue a life that you were made for. Do not let the past permanently weaken you. Please find the strength to move on. I urge you to seek guidance and counseling because everyone's healing journey will differ.

Before I leave you, I want to give you a mission. When you pursue healing and have gleaned all the knowledge you can from this book, pass it on. I want you to pay it forward with these words. Give this book away to someone who will benefit from it. I hope that someday I will see what God has done with these words given in my surrendering to Him.

Milton Keynes UK
Ingram Content Group UK Ltd.
UKHW012314060524
442290UK00005B/375